Tutus, Tights and Tiptoes

SOUND AND VISION

Tutus, Tights and Tiptoes

Ballet History as It Ought to Be Taught

David W. Barber

CARTOONS
Dave Donald

SOUND AND VISION

TABLE OF CONTENTS

Author's Note and Acknowledgements

IT WAS LIONEL KOFFLER, my distributing publisher at Firefly Books, who first suggested a book on ballet, so I thank him for the idea and for persisting through several earlier books until I got down to doing it.

And of course I'd like again to thank Geoff Savage at Sound And Vision Publishing for his friendship and all his hard work and dedication to the cause over the years. And thanks as always to Dave Donald, whose wonderful illustrations add so much to these books and whose good company always makes these projects more enjoyable. We three make a pretty good team, I think. Thanks also to Jacky Savage at Sound And Vision, for her help with the manuscript. And special thanks to my friend Alisa Walton, for her artistic advice and technical expertise.

AND TO YOU, THE READERS, I truly hope you enjoy this new book, and thanks for your support and kind words of the earlier ones. In particular, to any dancers out there, I hope you enjoy this book in the affectionate, if slightly irreverent, spirit in which it was written. The last thing I'd want to do with dancers is to step on any toes.

DWB
Toronto, 2000

PREFACE

E VEN THOUGH BALLET was started by wealthy aristo-crats who wanted entertainment at their parties, I've never been a snob about dance, and I don't think of it as an elitist art form. I think it's something everyone can appreciate and understand. That's one of the things I like so much about David Barber's *Tutus, Tights and Tiptoes*. This is history made fun.

When I was growing up and studying to be a dancer, I had snippets and bits of this. We knew about the ballerina who caught fire and how poor Tchaikovsky died thinking his incredible *Swan Lake* was a complete failure. But to find out so much more about these stories, and in the humorous way David tells them, makes them much more interesting, makes them all come alive. You get a sense these are real flesh-and-blood human beings who struggled and had failures and successes.

It's a fascinating history, and this is a book for people who want to know more about the history of dance without having to slog through all those highly academic volumes. I found it to be great fun, and educational as well.

I liked it a lot, I certainly learned a few things and I had some good laughs along the way.

Karen Kain
Toronto, August 2000

DEDICATION

To my parents,
Mollie Barber and the late Richard Campbell Barber,
whose obvious love of music — and humor —
first inspired my own.

The first dance

JUMPING IN
FEET FIRST

THE HISTORY OF DANCE goes all the way back before there was any history, if you see what I mean. That is to say, people have been dancing almost as long as there have been people at all. Anything before that gets just a little too confusing.

Dance historians and other scholars disagree over whether the kind of jumping up and down and prancing around done by horses, dogs, cattle and other animals should count as dancing for the purposes of the history books, and I'm afraid we're just going to have to let them keep arguing about it. For what it's worth, for the purposes of *this* history book, I'd be inclined to say that dogs and horses make pretty good dancers, but I'm not so sure about cattle. They're just generally too sluggish and ungraceful. Walt Disney's *Fantasia*, of course, gave us the image of dancing hippopotamuses (hippopotami?), but that's an animated cartoon and so doesn't really count in most scientific circles.

At any rate, dancing probably began when some prehistoric cave dweller stubbed a toe on a big rock by the campfire. Amazingly, this little scenario contains all the basic elements essential to dance — movement (jumping up and down), gesture (grasping the injured toe with both hands), special lighting (the campfire) and (if screams of agony count) some sort of musical accompaniment. Dressing rooms, box seats and exorbitant ticket prices probably came shortly thereafter. (Millions of years later, in works such as *Le Sacre du Printemps* and *Petrushka*, com-

1

poser Igor Stravinsky provided ballet music to accompany similar primitive gestures and movement. It's always good when an art form can get back to its roots.)

ONCE EARLY HUMANS ORGANIZED themselves into tribes, dancing became a more serious business, often with specific goals in mind. There were dances to inspire the soldiers before going into battle, dances to frighten the enemy and dances to console the survivors if the battle hadn't gone so well that day. There were dances to bring on rain (and probably others to say, "OK, we've had enough rain now, thanks"), dances to ensure good crops or plentiful hunting and fishing, and dances to celebrate marriages and births (often preferably in that order). Many tribal societies also developed a dance of death, or *danse macabre*, as a way of making the prospect of the afterlife a little less scary.[1]

Many religions around the world include dancing as part of their important rituals, whether to please or appease their various gods or just as a way to celebrate life. In India, Hindu teachings instruct that the world was created by a dancing god, Lord Shiva, which just goes to show how important they think it is. Christian sects, in fact — not all, but a stern few — are rare among world religions in considering dancing to be wicked, unacceptable and downright evil.[2]

THE ANCIENT GREEKS CONSIDERED dancing to be inspired by the gods and so put a lot of thought into the matter. They even developed a complex system combining rhythm and movement and called *cheironomia*, from the Greek word *cheir*, meaning hand. Dancing was presided over by Terpsichore, one of the nine Muses in charge of the various arts. In particular, there were two gods in charge of dance — Apollo, the sun god who also

---

[1] This doesn't always work, but at least it's worth a try.

[2] The old joke goes that Baptists forbid lovemaking standing up because it might lead to dancing.

looked after philosophy and art, and Dionysus, the god of wine, revelry, fertility and other wild abandon.[3]

Thus, even from ancient times, we can see that dance has been divided into two categories — the highbrow dancing of artistic expression and the lowbrow dancing of getting drunk and having a good time. We continue to maintain these distinctions even today. In general, ballet is considered a highbrow, artistic pursuit. (The drunkenness and sexual pursuit comes later, usually at the party *after* the performance.)

MANY OF THE BEST GREEK DANCES actually come from the island of Crete, whose people were conquered around 1400 B.C. or so by mainland Grecians from the city-state Mycenae, or Mycenaeans, who stole all the Cretans' best moves. Every once in a while, Mycenaean Greeks were known to burst into bouts of frenzied dancing, for reasons historians have been unable to determine (though it might have something to do with the wine — see above). Even today, there are still some cretins in the dance world, but that's something else again.

The ancient Greeks divided theatre into two types, comedy and tragedy. (The term tragedy comes from *tragoidia*, or "goat song," because Dionysus and followers of the ancient Mystery religions considered the goat a sacred animal).[4]

Dionysus is also sometimes known as Bacchus, from which we get the words bacchanalia and bacchanalian. Dionysus, or Bacchus, had a traumatic childhood. His mother, Semele, having been accidentally reduced to a pile of ashes by his father, Jove, Bacchus was instead born out of Jove's thigh. That sort of thing tends to have an effect, and would have made big headlines if the Greeks had had medical journals in those days. (Handel later

---

[3] People who can name the nine Muses are generally the same ones who can name all 12 apostles and all seven of Snow White's dwarves.

[4] This seems appropriate, since many in the theatre are old goats themselves and some performances can stink like a goat.

wrote a whole opera based on the Semele story, ash pile and all.)

EARLY GREEK THEATRE CONTAINS many of the elements associated with modern theatre in general, and in fact with ballet in particular. There was a chorus of dancers — all of them male, which meant that some men had to play the women's parts in the drama (thereby establishing a tradition of effeminate males in theatre that continues today). And to protect their feet on the rough ground of the outdoor amphitheatres, the performers wore little slippers not unlike those worn by ballet dancers today.

If I were more conscientious, I'd take the time now to discuss the Greek *dithyramb*, a song-and-dance routine accompanied by flute music. But I'm not and I'm not going to dither about the *dithyramb*. Take it from me, it's very important and you really should read up on it if you want your knowledge of Greek theatrical history to be well rounded. Me, I always like to leave a few rough edges.

THE ANCIENT GREEKS ALSO DEVELOPED a form of theatre later picked up on by the Romans (and much, much later by the English), known as the pantomime. This started off all right but later became lewd and sensational and generally got out of hand. Sometimes, condemned criminals were added to the cast and forced to dance near flames until their flammable clothing caught fire and they burned to death in front of the audience. What fun! Anything to please the crowd, I guess. You'd think some of them might have had the foresight to dunk their costumes in water before the show, but apparently not. (Ballet has a long tradition of setting fire to its performers. In 1393, the French king Charles VI had a close call when his costume caught fire, and in the 1800s a couple of Parisian dancers got too close to gaslamps on stage and likewise went up in flames, causing severe burns from which they later died. Among other things, dancers should always carry comprehensive fire insurance.)

4

DANCING WAS ALSO KNOWN in ancient Rome among Jews and early Christians, though much of the dancing mentioned in the Bible tends to turn out badly. Salome, for instance, danced at a birthday party for her stepfather, Herod, and what happened? John the Baptist wound up with his head on a plate.

King David mentions dancing often in his psalms, usually along with timbrels and tabrets — whatever they are. When David saw Bathsheba do a little soapy dance in the bathtub, he was so overcome with lust that he immediately slept with her and got her pregnant. Then he arranged to have her husband, Uriah the Hittite, conveniently killed in battle so he could marry her. To be fair to Bathsheba, all she was really trying to do was keep clean and build up a good lather. The story tells us that David's actions "displeased" God, though given that the *Book of Leviticus* instructs that all adulterers should be put to death, David got off rather lightly. Bit of a slipup there, if you ask me.[5]

JESUS AND HIS FOLLOWERS SEEM to have had little time for dancing, though given how many other details the Gospels scrimp on, I suspect there was rather more dancing going on than we're led to believe. Jesus himself, in popular folksong, is sometimes referred to as Lord of the Dance (a term much more recently applied to that popularlizer of Irish stepdancing, Michael Flatley — although I'd be careful of making too close a connection there).

There must have been dancing at the wedding feast in Cana of Galilee, for instance, especially after Jesus turned all that water into wine (see Dionysus, above). And personally, I think Mary Magdalene probably knew a few interesting steps or two, and so did that woman at Simon the Leper's house with the special ointment and the long hair — but that's just a theory.

---

5 David also dressed up in linen and did a little dance in front of the ark of the covenant, which may have helped put him back in God's good books.

Irish stepdance: marionettes with a few strings broken

FLINGS AND
OTHER THINGS

HISTORIANS AND ANTHROPOLOGISTS assure us there was probably dancing associated with the Druid rituals for the solstice or equinox and other sacred occasions at Stonehenge and elsewhere throughout ancient Britain of the Celts, though what evidence they base this on I'm not sure. No one at the time thought to make any recordings and a videotape of such rituals is not available in any stores. (If you find any ancient Druid videotapes for sale on eBay, if I were you I'd ask for an authentication sticker.)

Druids also gave us such traditions as holly, mistletoe and Christmas trees, not to mention Easter eggs. The early Christians were notorious for stealing some of their best bits from the Druids, and to this day they aren't even paying any royalties.

SPEAKING OF ROYALTY, although King Henry VIII became enormously fat in later life, in his youth he was a fine figure of a man known for his shapely legs and his athletic dancing skills – when he wasn't beheading his wives, of course. It's probably not true that Henry VIII wrote *Greensleeves* — he was more your ostentatious cloth of gold type — but he was known to have written a pretty good tune or two, so it's quite possible that some of the songs he liked to dance to at parties and other fancy court occasions were ones he composed himself.

Anne Boleyn, Henry's second wife and the first of two he beheaded, wrote a lovely song in the Tower of London while awaiting her execution, called *O Deathe, Rock Me Asleepe*. It's sort of a lullaby, but probably a little too morbid for you to be singing to your children.

(When he wasn't beheading wives, Henry could be quite charming when he wanted to be. When courting Anne Boleyn, Henry would tell her how much he loved her breasts, which he affectionately called her "sweet duckies." Later, when she had become a nuisance he wanted rid of, he accused her of having three breasts, an obvious sign of witchcraft. He was what you might call putting all his duckies in a row.)

Henry's daughter, Queen Elizabeth I, as a young woman caused a scandal at court for dancing *la volta*, a particularly risqué French dance of the 16th century that showed entirely too much leg. If Elizabeth were a young monarch today, she'd probably be all over the tabloids for dancing *la bamba* or living *la vida loca*. (Which by comparison would be a darn sight more discreet than some of the antics the modern Royals have been up to. I mean, really! This is what you get for letting cousins marry.) Elizabeth liked to start each morning with some aerobics by dancing a few lively galliards, just to get the blood going. Nowadays she'd be taking Tae-bo.[1]

AMONG THE DANCES ASSOCIATED with England is the tradition of Morris dancing, which is based on a Spanish dance with an Italian name that the English stole from the Burgundian French one day around 1420 or so. This dance was called the *moresca*, sometimes *morisca*, which probably comes from the Spanish word *morisco*, meaning "Moor," or possibly from the Greek word *moros*, meaning "fool." (The terms "dancer" and "fool" sometimes may or may not amount to the same thing). Its resem-

---

[1] The galliard comes from the Italian *gagliarda*. It's in 6/8 and you dance it a lot like the *saltarello*, except on the fifth beat you have to jump a little higher.

blance to the English word "morose" is probably just a coincidence.[2]

The name comes from the fact that some of the performers would dress up in blackface, which everybody thought was jolly fun (unless of course you are black to begin with, in which case it's just insulting). One old French version, for instance, known as the *danse des bouffons*, is meant to represent Christians fighting with Moors (who of course would be in blackface and therefore were considered the bad guys. It's all in your perspective.) In some early versions of the Herod story, Salome dances a *moresca* — with or without the seven veils.

A bunch of shepherds dance a little *moresca* at the end of Monteverdi's opera *Orfeo* (which is maybe where we get the expression "black sheep of the family"), and Mozart has a sort of *moresca* near the beginning of *Don Giovanni*, when the Don first meets Zarlina. And Shakespeare was probably familiar with the *moresca* tradition when he created Othello, the blackfaced Moor of Venice.[3]

At any rate, by the 15th century, it had come to be known in England as the Morris dance, which still survives today, although some of us wish it didn't. The Morris dance is a lively and frolicsome caper, usually in 2/4 time (but sometimes 3/4, just to see if everybody's paying attention), in which the dancers wear jangly bells attached to their legs. (When a Morris dancer tells you, "I'll be there with bells on," he actually means it. It's quite annoying, really.)

Morris dancing is done in May to celebrate the return of spring (which means at some level it's probably all tied in with

---

2 Pay attention, now: It's very important not to confuse the dancing *moresca* with its other musical counterpart, the *moresca* that's a variant of the *villanella*, a 16th-century version of the madrigal, only much more lewd and suggestive. This musical *moresca* comes from Naples and is — oh, never mind.

3 Desdemona "sings, plays and dances well," as Othello tells us in Act III scene iii, line 185.

the Druids and the vernal equinox), and involves a bunch of people getting together to dance around a maypole and create such silly characters as the Fool, Maid Marian, the Pantomime Horse and of course at least one poor fellow running around with charcoal or burnt cork rubbed on his face. (Al Jolson hadn't been invented yet, but you know we'll get there eventually.)

(Beyond Morris dancing, there's all sorts of leftover pagan stuff lying around. In fact, many people don't like to admit it, but Christianity is full of pagan influences. The star and the shepherds at Christmas, the manger, the holly and the mistletoe and the Christmas tree, the palm leaves and the donkey on Palm Sunday, the whole Easter resurrection thing — oh, don't even get me started.)

ELSEWHERE IN BRITAIN, the Scots were having fun in their own way tossing the caber (not to be confused with the caper, which is either a lively dance, a jewel heist or a spicy pickled garnish for salads and pasta dishes). The Scots also developed the Highland Fling, which is different from the sort of lowlife fling you might find yourself in after getting all Dionysian and drinking too much wine.

And, speaking of Celts and silly dancing, the Irish meanwhile were busy developing stepdancing. The Welsh are generally better known for their singing than their dancing, dancing being a little more difficult to do when you're down the bottom of a coal mine. "On the whole," we can imagine a Welshman saying, "I'd rather have been a dancer than a miner." It's dark, down the mine, for one thing, not to mention crowded. (Though, come to think of it, they'd have an easy time doing the blackface routine, what with all that coal dust just lying around.)

The Irish stepdance, in our own time made popular by *Riverdance* and Michael Flatley (see Lord of the Dance, back in Chapter 1) involves a lot of fancy footwork while keeping the upper body stiff as a board, arms down at the sides. (The

Scots fling their arms up in the air, which somehow seems more natural.) A lot of people seem to love it, but to me, that Irish bit always looks faintly ridiculous, as if the dancers were marionettes with a few strings broken. Or maybe just a few screws loose.

Stepping up to the barre

GETTING FRENCHED

WE TEND TO THINK OF BALLET as French, but of course the Italians will tell you they thought of it first. And of course to that the French would reply, with typical Gallic *savoir faire* and slipping easily into the *subjonctif*, that even if that were so, it's the French who've raised ballet to such *merveilleux* heights as an art form.

They'd go on arguing like this for days if you'd let them, but naturally we haven't time for that. So let's just say they're both right as far as they go and try to move on to more important things, shall we?

THE TRUTH IS THAT in the 14th and 15th centuries, the royal courts of France, Italy and Burgundy all were renowned for their fine dancing and entertainment. (Burgundy was more or less a separate country in those days, or at least a duchy, and not just a color or a fine wine.) And if you had a princedom or a dukedom or some other chunk of land you were lording it over and you wanted to impress all your vassals and peasants, not to mention the neighbors, with how important you were (and who doesn't?), you simply had to put on a fancy do with dining and drinking and dancing. It got to be that you just weren't *anybody* unless you could put on a good show.

Most of these spectacles took place for special occasions, although sometimes any old occasion would do. So a wedding or a holiday feast or some visiting bigshot in town would certainly do the trick. In 1393, for instance, Charles VI of France put on a little costume ball, or *mascarade*, he called the *Bal des Ardens*, in which Charles and a few of his noble friends got into the spirit of things by dressing up as savages in a chain gang, all linked together and covered in black tar and cloth. (It was one of those blackface *moresca* dances we talked about last chapter. And as to why it's *Bal* and not *Ball*, don't ask me. Ask Charles.)

Anyway, as Charles and co. were trooping in, it seems the Duc d'Orleans leaned forward with a lit torch to get a closer look and, oops, set everyone on fire. Now, he claims it was just an accident and the fact that he was the king's brother and might have stood to inherit the throne was entirely a coincidence. Well, sure. Who are we to argue?

Charles might indeed have been fried to a crisp except that just a moment before he'd slipped out of his chains and waltzed over to flirt with the Duchess of Berry, who helpfully protected him from the flames by letting him hide under her dress. A sort of a king *à la* chicken, you might say. At least, that's what the Duchess of Berry *said* was going on. All the other noblemen died in the ensuing fire, except one who had the presence of mind to jump into a nearby tub of water. (Some noblemen are just smarter than others. Others marry their cousins and it all just goes downhill from there.)

Most of these dancing events started off small, relatively speaking, and certainly far less traumatic, with just the ordinary sort of dancing you'd find at royal courts. But pretty soon, you know how it goes, things started getting more elaborate and before you knew it, they'd gotten quite out of hand. They started adding fancy scenery, and more elaborate costumes, and little plot lines to give the story some substance, and the orchestra playing the music kept getting bigger and bigger. When Charles VIII of France crossed the Alps to get to Naples he saw some pretty spiffy stuff. One production put on by the Duke of Milan in 1496, for instance, had costumes and stage effects and whizbang machinery all designed by no less than Leonardo da Vinci, who had to be doing *something* to keep busy when he wasn't designing flying machines or building catapults or writing back-wards in his notebooks or painting the Mona Lisa.

And with these elaborate productions came the emergence of the professional dance master, or what nowadays we'd call a choreographer. Among the first and most important of these was Domenico di Piacenza, who worked for the Estes, one of the richest and therefore most powerful families knocking around Ferrara. Sometime around 1400, in fact, Domenico wrote what may be the first treatise on dancing, in which he actually wrote down notation on how the dance steps were to be performed. There'd already been musical notation since about 800 or so, but it's relatively straightforward compared to figuring out how to notate physical movement. Some of Domenico's other dances were also later notated around 1450 by his pupils Antonio Cornazano and William the Jew.

Cornazano worked for the Sforzas, who were bigshots in Milan, whereas William the Jew (or Guglielmo Ebreo, as he was known in Italian) tended to move around more, since he was obviously talented and much in demand. He was what you might call — sorry, can't resist — a wandering Jew.

At any rate, William's employers included Lorenzo the Magnificent, who was part of the Medici clan in Florence, and Galeazzo Sforza, the Duke of Milan. William was later even knighted in Venice by the Holy Roman Emperor. (I'm pretty sure that would be Sigismund of Hungary and Bohemia, who got the job in 1433 from Pope Eugene IV, but I have trouble keeping track and quite frankly it hardly seems worth worrying about.)[1]

The sorts of dances Domenico di Piacenza and Cornazano and William the Jew were creating had little stories, often loose-ly based on Greek myths (or based on loose Greek myths), about

---

[1] I also feel constrained to remark at this point, as Voltaire has noted, that the Holy Roman Emperor is neither Holy, nor Roman, nor even an Emperor. But hey, that's the title that comes with the job.

15

several rival men fighting for the affections of the same young woman. They came to be known as *balli*, or *balletti*, from the Italian word *ballare*, meaning "to dance." From there, of course, we get the French term *ballet*.[2]

Now, don't go confusing "ballet" with "ballett" (or *balletto* in Italian), which is the rather obscure technical term in English for the kind of madrigal with a repeating "fa-la-la" refrain. It's only the really pedantic who worry about this sort of thing, by the way. Most people just call them all madrigals and have done with it. It saves time. The well-known Christmas song that goes "Deck the hall with boughs of holly ..." is a ballett, with nothing whatsoever to do with ballet. I'm sure its reference to "gay apparel" is entirely a coincidence.[3]

BY THE 16TH CENTURY all sorts of interesting things were happening, dance-wise. Dance steps were getting more intricate and dancing instructors began to advise their pupils to practise the tougher moves by hanging on to the back of a chair or a taut rope for balance and support. From this we get the ballet *barre*, the wooden or metal rail found in almost every ballet classroom — not to mention many strip clubs (or so they tell me), but that's another matter.

Knowing how to dance was considered one of the essential elements of any lady or gentleman's proper education, right up there with knowing which fork to use for the fish or knowing how to fence, play tennis or ride a horse. In 1588, a writer named Thoinot Arbeau (really a French priest named Jehan

---

[2] Interestingly, *ballare* can sometimes mean "wobble." And the Italian word *balla* can mean "rubbish" or "nonsense" — but there's probably no connection there.

[3] Also, don't confuse *ballet* and *ballett* and *balletto* with the *ballata*, one of the chief forms of Italian vocal music of the 14th-century Ars Nova. The *ballata*, as the *Harvard Dictionary of Music* so helpfully points out, "is not related to the French *ballade* but is practically identical with the *virelai*, which was also called *chanson balladée*." There. Clear as mud.

Tabourot) wrote a book called *Orchésographie*, which is chock-full of useful information. In the form of dialogues, Arbeau instructs his dim-witted pupil Capriol (playing the straight man) in such social niceties as proper dancing and when to blow your nose in public.

"Spit and blow your nose sparingly," Arbeau advises, "or if needs must, turn your head away and use a fair white handkerchief." Words to live by, even today. (Though it's not surprising why Tabourot used a pseudonym. I would have, too.)

Speaking of horses, even they were getting into the act, with what the Italians called *balletti a cavallo* and the French called *carrousels* or *danses equestres* — which by any other name we would call a horse ballet.

Horses, as you probably know, can be quite intelligent (though some horses can be about as dumb as the rest of us) and they generally respond quite well to training. So with enough work and the right riders, horses can be taught to perform complex and beautiful dance routines, though getting them to stand on their tippytoes has always been a bit of a problem. The most famous dancing horses are of course the Lipizzaner Stallions of Vienna — who, for reasons best known to people other than myself, live in Austria but are members of a Spanish riding school. And this was long before the European Union. They still dance today, on tour around the world and at home in Vienna in a lovely theatre/stables complex built for them in 1729.[4]

Whether teaching horses to dance is really worth all the effort is another question, and one I'd just as soon leave for another day. At any rate, at least horses are a lot easier to train for dancing than, say, rhinoceroses or even elephants. Igor Stravinsky once wrote a polka for 50 circus elephants, the sort of

---

[4] Despite diligent research, I have been unable to confirm whether the tradition of horse ballets has anything to do with the tradition of calling dancers "hoofers." I'll get back to you on that if anything comes up.

commission that doesn't come along every day. A pachyderm polka, you might call it.[5]

ALSO IN THE 16TH CENTURY, the French were really getting into the swing of things. When Catherine de'Medici married King Henri II of France in 1533, their wedding spectacle was, well, pretty spectacular. (Henri, by the way, wasn't yet a king when Catherine married him. He was only a duke, but she soon fixed that.) Catherine was Italian and rich and sophisticated and liked the finer things in life and didn't mind that everyone knew it. She liked lovely dresses and big mirrors and was largely responsible for introducing white face powder to French society. Today we call it the Goth look.

After Henri II, the job of king went to Charles IX and then Henri III, his sons by Catherine de'Medici. And although she wasn't actually on the throne, she was certainly the power behind it. Sure, Chuck or Hank may have had the title, but Mama Kate was really the one in charge. And don't you forget it.

Along with the face powder and the dresses and all the other items Catherine had imported from Italy was a fellow who became her valet, Baltazarini di Belgiojoso, or Baldassare de Belgioioso — or, as he became known in French, Balthasar de Beaujoyeulx. Aside from being a capable valet, Beaujoyeulx was also an accomplished violinist, a graceful dancer and an impressive choreographer. (And if he was good in other areas that Catherine might have come to appreciate, what business is it of ours?)

In 1573, Beaujoyeulx created *Le Ballet des Polonais* to impress the visiting Polish ambassador, complete with music by Orlando

---

[5] Although pachyderm is a term most people use, if they use it at all, to mean only elephants, in fact all sorts of animals are pachyderms — meaning they have four hoofed feet and thick skins. Horses and rhinos are actually pachyderms too, and so are pigs. Cows and camels don't count because they chew their cuds and have too many stomachs. Now you know.

di Lasso and poems by Pierre Ronsard.[6] But for our purposes, his most important accomplishment was the creation of a dance spectacle he called the *Balet comique de la Royne*, for the wedding of Marguerite of Lorraine-Vaudémont, sister of Henri III's wife, Queen Louise, to the Duc de Joyeuse. It may have been only her son's wife's sister, but Catherine de'Medici decided that the wedding was going to be one humdinger of a show. And that it was, thanks largely to the efforts of Beaujoyeulx, and a whole lot of cash from Catherine.

Even though it was called *"comique,"* it wasn't even remotely funny, though today we might consider it all a bit ridiculous. The French terms *comique* and *comédie* refer not specifically to comedy but to drama in general. Don't ask me why. The French are just funny that way. At any rate, Catherine must have been pleased by the results, because after the show she let all of Europe know about it by sending out letters complete with glowing descriptions and fancy illustrations. Nowadays she'd be one of those people posting baby pictures and postcards on her Web page, www.catherinedemedici.com

The big event took place in the Salle du Bourbon one fall day in 1581, and anybody who was *anybody* was there — including, of course, the bride and groom and King Henri III and his wife, Queen Louise, the bride's sister, who made her entrance in a golden carriage spouting water. (The carriage was spouting water, not Louise.) The plot had something to do with the Greek myth of Circe, but nobody was really paying much attention to that. All they really cared about was the dancing and the costumes. And, of course, being seen.

The whole thing lasted nearly six hours and didn't wrap up until 3 in the morning. by which time everyone was pretty

---

[6] Not that it has anything to do with anything except it's interesting, but "polish/Polish" is the only word in the English language that changes its pronunciation when you capitalize the first letter. It doesn't work the same way in French, so the Polish ambassador wouldn't have been impressed by that.

much exhausted. Beaujoyeulx's choreography involved a lot of dancers moving in intricate patterns that were best appreciated from above, which is where the audience members were sitting, in galleries surrounding the floor. Imagine a 16th-century version of those old Hollywood Busby Berkeley movie musicals of the 1930s.

FRANCE IN THE 17TH CENTURY has been called "The Golden Age of Ballet," and never more often than by the French themselves. Composers Pierre Guédron, Antoine Boësset, Jean de Cambefort and their crowd were writing *ballets de cour*, or court ballets — similar to the English masque, which Ben Jonson and Inigo Jones had a hand in, as you may know (and if you don't, well, sorry, we don't have time to stop for that now).[7]

Presiding over this "golden age" was Louis XIV, who was born in 1638 and reigned from 1643 till his death in 1715, after which he no longer felt up to the job. Most of us think of Louis XIV, if we think of him at all, as he was later in his reign — building Versailles and other fancy palaces and stuffing them full of mistresses and illegitimate children (12 of 'em) and Louis Quatorze furniture, invading Flanders and the Low Countries, revoking the Edict of Nantes, thereby forcing the Huguenots to leave France and firmly laying a foundation for the French Revolution in 1789, and generally messing things up all around.[8]

But it's well to remember that before becoming a crotchety old man, Louis was once just a kid who liked nothing more than

---

[7] English historians tend to go on about how important the masque was. But really, in the grand scheme of things, and especially in the history of ballet, it's merely a blip.

[8] Louis's predecessor, Henri IV, had passed the Edict of Nantes in 1598, which gave the Huguenots and other French Protestants the right to religious freedom. Although by this time a Catholic himself, Henri may have felt he owed it to them, since before that when he'd been plain old Henri of Navarre he'd been a Huguenot himself. Anyway, Louis XIV ruined all that.

to have a good time.[9] Even more than invading the Low Countries, and maybe even more than all his mistresses, Louis loved ballet. In 1651, when he was just a little tad of 12 or so (and before most of the mistresses and illegitimate kiddies came along), Louis danced in his first ballet, *Cassandre*, and from then on he was hooked. In fact, he probably took it all a little bit too seriously. After performing roles such as the sun god Apollo and the Rising Sun (in *Ballet de la Nuit*), Louis began to think of himself as Louis *le Roi Soleil*, or "Louis the Sun King." (Some people had other names for him, but we'd best not mention them in polite company.)[10]

Louis eventually had to stop dancing because he became too fat, but before that he learned some of his best moves from the foremost dancing teacher of the day, Pierre Beauchamps. Among other things, Beauchamps helped develop standards for the five basic positions of the feet, some of which have their origins in the traditional stances of fencing. (See, I *told* you fencing was important!)

Louis made other contributions to the arts. In 1661 he founded the Académie Royale de Danse, whose teachers were officially headquartered in the Louvre, but who generally liked to get together in a local pub nearby. And in 1669, Louis established the Académie Royale de Musique, which remains today as the Paris Opéra and which started out in a leaky, drafty old tennis court before later moving to a nicer spot.

THE MOST IMPORTANT COMPOSER in the court of Louis XIV was Jean-Baptiste Lully (1632-87). He was originally an Italian, Giovanni Battista (or sometimes Giambattista) Lulli, a poor

---

[9] Cardinal Richelieu had helped organize a pretty fancy ballet when Louis XIV was born.

[10] An Italian visitor once remarked that Louis knew as much about music as he did about military tactics, but he was wrong. Louis knew a lot more about music.

Florentine miller's son, and therefore as good an example as any of the French/Italian crossover we mentioned at the start of the chapter.

He was also a good example of how to get ahead in the world, thanks to talent and more than a little intrigue. Brought to France by the Chevalier de Guise as a boy of 14 to help Mademoiselle de Monpensier learn Italian, pretty soon Lully had become her *valet de chambre* and by 1652 had joined the king's court. By 1653 he was dancing alongside the king in the *Ballet de la Nuit*, for which he had composed much of the music (along with Cambefort), and *Le Marriage de Thétis et Peleus*. Louis soon appointed him *compositeur de la musique instrumentale* – or for those not quite bilingual, court composer of instrumental music.[11]

Somewhere along the way — don't ask me where — Lully the violinist had learned to dance and he performed in some 30 ballets at the court. But more important, he composed the music for ballets — 28 or so, ending with *Le Temple de la paix* in 1685 — not to mention operas, incidental music for plays and other instrumental music, choral works and who knows what else. Lully could be witty and charming, but he was also a liar, a cheat and a control freak. A jealous rival named Guichard once tried to murder him using a poisoned snuff box, but those sorts of things never work the way they should.

Lully helped introduce ballet as a regular feature in operas of the day, and with the famous French playwright Molière helped create the *comédie-ballet* in such works as *Les Amans Manifiques* and *Le Bourgeois Gentilhomme*. (Molière died in 1673, just hours after performing the lead role his play *Le Malade imaginaire*, or *The Imaginary Invalid*. Obviously, it wasn't so

---

[11] Louis XIV liked Lully so much in part because Lully could make him laugh until he cried. Louis was big on pratfalls, and Lully was happy to oblige. Once, just to amuse the king, Lully jumped onto a harpsichord and smashed it to bits.

imaginary after all.) These *comédie-ballet* productions, with dance numbers interspersed among the dialogue, could be considered the forerunners of present-day Broadway-style musicals. So if you feel like blaming Lully for *Annie* or *Oklahoma!* or even *Cats*, go right ahead.[12]

But bad musicals aside, we have other reasons to be upset about Lully. Although in 1662 he married Madeleine, the daughter of court composer Michel Lambert, and with her had six children, and although he seems in many respects to have been a decent husband and father, there's just no getting around the fact that, in his spare time, Lully was a notorious pedophile. For him, the phrase "consenting adults" seems not to have entered the vocabulary.

So if it's all the same to you, I'd just as soon not say much more about Lully, except to note that he died infamously and ignominiously on the 22nd of March, 1687, after having stubbed his toe with a large staff he was using to beat time for a performance of a *Te Deum* to celebrate the king's recovery from an illness. Lully bashed his toe, he got gangrene and he died. And it serves him right, too.

---

12 Molière was a pseudonym, too, by the way. His real name was Jean-Baptiste Poquelin.

Precise timing in the Minute Minuet

WITH YOU IN
A MINUET

ONE OF THE MOST IMPORTANT and popular dances at this time was the minuet (or in French, *menuet*), a lightweight little ditty Lully introduced around 1650 or so. It's not clear where he got the idea, but he probably stole it from somewhere. I wouldn't put it past him.[1]

Louis XIV, of course, takes credit for dancing the first "official" minuet, in 1653 they say, and since he was king we'd better let him. Pretty soon the minuet had become the hottest dance craze of the late 17th and early 18th centuries — right up there with the foxtrot and the jitterbug later on and even bigger than the macarena is today. (Or was. The macarena's so *passé* now, you know? Like, where have you *been?*)

Like the waltz (which became the big thing in salons later in the 18th century, thanks to the father/son team named Johann Strauss), the minuet is in 3/4 time. You dance it in a Z- or S-shaped pattern, depending on whether you're a stickler for details or you like cutting corners. Louis, who was definitely a corner-cutter, liked the minuet so much he made it the "official" court dance at Versailles, or wherever Louis happened to be hanging out at the moment.

The minuet soon swept Europe (which needed a good cleaning anyway) and, like crabgrass or purple loosestrife, pretty soon it had taken over and crowded out many of the other pop-

---

1 Some scholars believe the minuet comes from an earlier French country dance form, the *branle à mener*, or the *branle gay*. Sounds about right.

ular dance forms of the day, such as the *courante*, the *pavane*, the *bourée* and the *gavotte*.

Lully introduced the minuet into his ballets, operas and other instrumental music, and later it began showing up in the instrumental suites of composers such as Johann Pachelbel (and you thought all he wrote was that famous *Canon*). Those other dances also survived in instrumental suites and elsewhere (Telemann wrote *courantes*, and even Bach wrote a *bourée* or two), but at the French court especially, the minuet was all the rage.

To play this and other music, Louis founded *Les Petits Violons*, a string orchestra to rival the already established *24 Violons du Roi*. The name's a bit misleading, actually. Although *Les Petits Violons* was indeed a small ensemble, the violins themselves weren't petite at all. They were just the regular size.[2]

The minuet even worked its way into symphonies. Holzbauer, Stamitz and those others guys in the Mannheim School loved it almost as much as they liked the Mannheim steamroller, as did Haydn and Mozart (though "the statement that Haydn was the first to introduce the minuet into the symphony" says the *Harvard Dictionary of Music*, somewhat sternly, "is far from correct."). Mozart has a minuet in the Act I masquerade scene of his opera *Don Giovanni*. Later on, especially in symphonies, where it's usually the third movement, the minuet kept getting faster and faster. By the time Beethoven came along, it had turned into a scherzo, which is a whole different thing.[3]

In English we spell it minuet, sometimes menuet. In German it's *Menuett* and in Italian, *minuetto*. But it's never spelled

---

[2] Maybe the players were small.

[3] For a more complete and informative discussion of the Mannheim School and the development of symphonic form in the 18th century, please see that inestimable work of music scholarship *If It Ain't Baroque: More Music History as It Ought to Be Taught*. Or there are a few other books on the subject, too.

"menuit," except by accident. And "minute" means something else again. Interestingly, although Chopin later wrote a *Minute Waltz*, he apparently never thought to compose a *Minute Minuet*.

The pirouette

Tutu Much

WHEN LOUIS XIV ESTABLISHED the Paris Opéra in that rundown old tennis court in 1669, he really got the ball rolling (pardon the pun) for "traditional" ballet as we know it today. The company had its first production in 1671 with composer Robert Cambert's opera *Pomone*, which featured dances choreographed by Pierre Beauchamps. (He's the feet positions guy, remember?)

Knowing a good thing when he saw one, and never one to pass up an opportunity for self-advancement, Lully soon took over the Opéra and moved it to much nicer digs at the Palais Royale. Of course, that meant turfing out all the actors his old collaborator Molière had hired, but that sort of thing never seemed to bother Lully very much. He had a cast-iron heart. After all, what were a few more unemployed actors? By 1713, the Paris Opéra had established a separate dance school, which meant a lot of people were spending a long day at the *barre* before spending their nights at the bar.

UP UNTIL THIS TIME, the dancers on stage were men most of the time. I mean, most of the time they were men. What I really mean is, the men were men all of the time (well, most of them were, anyway) but sometimes they dressed up as women.[1]

Anyway, the point is that until this time, although women were allowed to dance socially in fancy balls at court or else-

---

[1] On stage, that is. Who knows what they did at home?

where, it still wasn't considered very proper or ladylike for women to dance on stage. In certain uppity circles, the theatre was considered too risqué even for men. It got so bad that to correct a shortage of good dancers, Louis XIV had to pass a royal decree allowing that courtiers could dance on stage without losing their noble rank or suffering social stigma. After all, he was the king and *he* danced, so how bad could it be?[2]

So before this, as in the plays of Shakespeare, female roles in ballets had been performed by young men or boys in drag ("*en travesti*," as they say in French, and some people call that a travesty). Since everybody was still wearing masks, for both male and female roles, this made it a lot easier to get away with. Men in female roles wore a short hooped skirt called a *tonnelet*. (Literally, "little cask." A cask of what, I'm not sure.)

But in the 1680s this began to change, and women began to be seen dancing on the French stage. They wore masks too, and a hooped skirt or dress called a *pannier*. (We haven't quite got to the modern tutu, but we're close.) The pannier was longer than the man's tonnelet, since most of the fancy jumping around and showoffy legwork was still being done by the male dancers. Everybody was also wearing silk stockings, the early equivalent of the modern tights, which hadn't been invented yet. There were also changes happening to footwear, but we'll deal with those later. (And if you'd like, we can get into a big argument over who invented tights. The candidates are dancer and stage effects creator Charles-Louis Didelot, hosiery maker Maillot, or trapeze artist Jules Léotard. I don't have a preference myself.)

Then in 1681, in what we might call a breakthrough for *liberté*, *egalité* and *sororité*, four women, the first ballerinas, danced for the production of Lully's opera *Le Triomphe de l'Amour*. So their leader, Mademoiselle de la Fontaine, could be considered

---

[2] When Molière lay on his deathbed, a celebrated playwright and man of letters, his friends couldn't find a priest to give him the last rites, because he was also an actor. Or maybe because he'd married the daughter of his mistress.

the first *prima ballerina* of the Paris Opéra, which pretty much makes her the first *prima ballerina* ever. Unfortunately for posterity, we know very little about Mlle. de la Fontaine, not even her first name. Someone get onto that, would you? Some scholars say that among the other dancers was a Mademoiselle des Mastins, who'd started out washing dishes in a restaurant, became a singer after she'd grown too fat to dance and eventually died of eating way too much.

It's ONE OF THOSE CURIOSITIES of the English language, by the way, that although we have the widely accepted word "ballerina" to describe a female ballet dancer, there's no such equivalent for the men. The only thing to call a male ballet dancer is, um, a male ballet dancer. (Well, you can call him a few other things, but they're generally considered impolite.) Following the example of alumnus and alumna, you'd think it would be ballerinus, or something. Of course, the term actually comes from the Italian, not the earlier Latin. Otherwise, the plural of ballerina wouldn't be ballerinas, it would be ballerinae — which of course it isn't. The generic term for dancer in Italian is either *danzatore* or *danzatrice* (in French *danseur/danseuse*, in German *Tänzer/Tänzerin*), but that's not quite the same somehow. Anyway, for some reason, even though Italian does have the term *ballerino* for a male dancer, only the feminine form has made its way (her way?) into English usage. Go figure.

And while we're on the topic of language, how come the fancy-dancy term for a gung-ho ballet fan is "balletomane" and not "balletophile"? Come to that, how come you never hear the term "operamane" or "symphonomane"? Of course, you don't even hear "operaphile" or "symphonophile" either. Oh, who knows? All it proves is that English is a crazy, illogical, inconsistent language. But we knew that already.

THE INTRODUCTION OF WOMEN to the stage coincided with the development of the *opera-ballet* — which, as its name suggests, was a theatrical production in which both music and dancing played important parts. Among the best-known of these was *Les Indes Gallantes*, by composer Jean-Philippe Rameau, first produced in 1735. And very elaborate it was, with designer Jean Nicholas Servandoni creating a wonderful erupting volcano for one scene.[3]

As this art form began to catch on, composer André Campra (whose own works include the opera-ballet *L'Europe Galante*) was heard to say that the best way to make it even more popular was to make the dances longer and women's skirts shorter. Even back then, they knew that sex sells. He'd fit right into Hollywood today.

Just as Beauchamps had codified the five basic positions of the feet (methodically numbered *première* through *cinquième*), ballet also began to develop terms for other basic "positions" (of the arms, of the legs, of the head) and poses, or "attitudes."[4]

About this time too we begin to formalize much of the specialized terminology for the leaps, turns, stances and other moves associated with ballet. France being the predominant centre for ballet (though the Italians would still argue the point), French terminology has become the standard form, just as Italian is the language used for highbrow music in other fields. (There. Call it a draw.) So the 18th century standardized such terms as *pas de deux* (literally "step of two," a dance for two people), *pirouette* (for a turn or whirl), *entrechats* (which looks like it should mean "between cats," but refers to a rapid fluttering of the legs), *fondue* (literally, sinking down or melting) and others such as *fouetté, jeté, plié, relevé* and *tombé*.[5]

---

[3] Before this, any eruptions on stage tended to be just the artists blowing up or letting off steam.

[4] Some people complain that dancers have only two attitudes — bad or indifferent.

[5] "The development of ballet would be substantially different without the influence of the French 'e' with an acute accent." Discuss in 500 words or less, for 20 marks.

ALTHOUGH BALLET WAS STILL very much a man's world, women began to have an influence not only as dancers but also as choreographers and teachers. Among the first of these was Françoise Prévost, who choreographed and danced the famous *Les Caractères de la Danse* in 1715, a series of solos based on popular dances of the day and addressed to the God of Love.[6]

Two of her pupils, Camargo and Sallé, became the most celebrated ballerinas of their generation, and they couldn't have been more different from each other if they'd tried.

Marie-Anne Cupis de Camargo was born in Brussels but seems to have inherited some of her grandmother's fiery Spanish blood. She was a real pistol, and even at her stage debut in 1726 was so impressive that Prévost immediately had her banished to the back row of the chorus, or *corps de ballet*, thus establishing a time-honored tradition of dealing with young rivals that continues to this day.

But one night one of the male dancers (it was either David Dumoulin or his brother, what's his name, the other one) missed his cue. Camargo saw her chance, leapt to the front of the stage and danced his solo. Well, the crowd loved her and Prévost was forced in embarrassment to retire shortly thereafter. Prévost also refused to give her any more lessons, so Camargo studied instead with male dancers including Dupré and Blondy, a nephew of Beauchamps.

Voltaire once said Camargo was the first ballerina to dance like a man, which he meant as a compliment. What he meant was her style was energetic, forceful and full of the leaping around and fancy footwork that until this time had been pretty much done only by the men. Camargo was probably the first female dancer to do those flutter-kick *entrechats*, for instance, and she even shortened her skirts a few inches to better show off her legs while she was doing them. No fool, she.

---

[6] I once tried addressing the God of Love. The letter came back "Return to Sender: Address Unknown."

Speaking of famous firsts, The first female pirouette was performed by the German ballerina Anne Heinel, who married the famous French dancer Gaétan Vestris. Their son Auguste was also a famous dancer, who came to be known as "Grandpapa Zephyr."

Camargo attracted many admirers and more than a few lovers, retired in 1751 with a huge pension and spent her later years lounging at her home on Rue Saint-Honoré, surrounded by dogs and cats and parrots and pigeons — and a bunch of jewelry and a pretty fine wine cellar, too.

MARIE SALLÉ, BY CONTRAST, was much quieter and less flashy. Where Camargo's dancing style was lively and flamboyant, Sallé's was more graceful and expressive. And where Camargo loved the lavish gifts and attention of a host of male admirers and lovers, Sallé was more modest and apparently turned down any lovers who approached her. She just wanted to dance.[7]

Sallé danced in Paris and London as a very young girl and made her official debut at the Paris Opéra in 1727, a year after Camargo, though legend has it that in 1721, in true theatrical fashion, she had once earlier filled in for Prévost when the older dancer was too sick to go on. The crowd loved her, too — and Prévost wasn't very happy about that, let me tell you.

But for all her shy, quiet demeanor, Sallé was no pushover and she knew what she wanted. Twice she quit the Paris Opéra in frustration and disgust over "artistic differences." The second time they'd have thrown her in jail (the rules were much more strict back then), so with her brother she escaped across the Channel to London in 1725, where she danced at Covent Garden.[8]

---

[7] Well, there were those rumors of her affair with the ballerina Manon Grognet, but that was probably just talk.

[8] She wasn't the only one with a temper. An earlier Opéra dancer, Marie-Thérèse Perdou de Subligny, once dumped a chamberpot on the head of the violinist Louis Francouer.

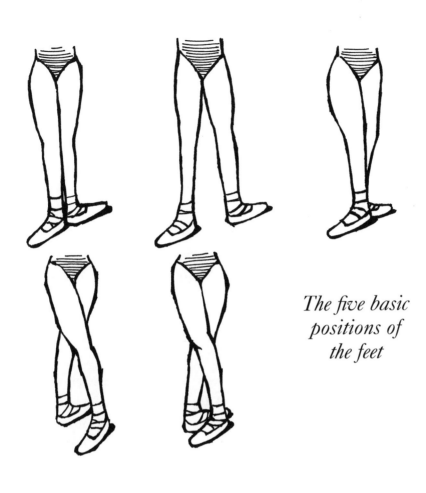

The five basic positions of the feet

Some positions not worth trying

Sallé created dances for *Il Pastor Fido, Alcina* and several other Handel operas, danced in pantomimes created by John Rich (who with John Gay created the famous *Beggar's Opera* in 1728) and in 1729 back in Paris caused a bit of a stir by dancing her own version of Prévost's *Les Caractères*, this time as a *pas de deux* with Antoine Lavale, without wearing any masks.

But that was nothing compared to the scandal of her version of *Pygmalion* in 1734 at the Drury Lane Theatre — which opened on Valentine's Day, appropriately enough. The story, you'll remember, is of a Greek sculptor who falls in love with the statue he's created of a beautiful woman, Galatea. In order to best represent the simple, flowing lines of a Greek statue, Sallé ditched the bulky old pannier dress and appeared instead in just a plain white cotton dress, slippers without heels, no mask, no jewelry and with her long hair worn down and flowing about her shoulders. Well, this was the closest the London audiences had ever come to seeing what today we might call an exotic dancer, and there were crowds lining up and rioting in the streets trying to get tickets. The scalpers were doing a brisk business.

BUT SOON, BARELY IN HER 30S, even Sallé was considered too old and she was overshadowed by a beautiful, hot Italian ballerina named Barbera Campanini, known by her stage name of La Barberina.

Barberina (no relation to me, alas) leapt higher, twirled faster and generally outdanced just about everybody. If Camargo had an *entrechat quatre*, Barberina could toss off an *entrechat huit* with no problem. She was typical of the Italian dancing style, generally more athletic than the French, which stresses grace and elegance. Like Camargo (but not Sallé), Barberina had a slew of lovers and it wasn't long before King Frederick the Great of Prussia had moved her to a fancy flat in Berlin as his official mistress. That was strictly for show, though, since most of the time Frederick just liked playing the flute and didn't actually much care for women at all. It just wasn't in his nature. (In today's

Hollywood parlance, she'd be known as his "beard.")

La Barberina spent her last years in repentance trying to make up for her wild, carefree life from before. She died at the age of 78 in 1799 after becoming the abbess of a convent she'd founded, which is about as repentant as you can get.[9]

BY THE 1770S, DANCERS HAD STOPPED wearing masks and wigs, their costumes had become much less cumbersome and flamboyant, the skirts shorter and looser, and over all things were looking pretty much the way they are in the "old-fashioned" ballets of today.

Through the 18th century there was also a push away from the *divertissements* or *ballets à entrées* that were just a bunch of unrelated showpieces strung together and often stuck in the middle of an opera, and a move toward what came to be called the *ballet d'action*, or action ballet, a unified ballet that actually tells a complete story. And instead of being just window dressing for an opera or some other musical form, often with words, ballets were starting to become wordless performances in their own right.[10]

Two rival ballet masters helped champion the *ballet d'action* in the 1750s and '60s, Gaspero Angiolini and Jean-Georges Noverre. Oh, they'd argue sometimes over who thought of it first, but really neither of them was right. As early as 1714, the Duchess of Maine had produced a little ballet completely in mime for some of her rich friends at her chateau at Sceaux, just outside Paris. The dancers were Françoise Prévost and Jean Balon, the play was Corneille's *Les Horaces* and the music was specially composed by Jean Joseph Mouret. Everything was lovely, the guests had a wonderful time, but it never really caught on. They just thought she was an eccentric old rich lady

---

[9] Frederick himself had died at 74 in 1786, unrepentant to the end.

[10] Later on we have the *Rite of Spring*, which is a whole different story.

having some fun. And they were probably right. (Many people, by the way, think that the term *ballon*, which refers to the lightness or spring in a dancer's step, comes from Jean Balon. But they're wrong about that. The Bournonville slipper, however, a big deal in all those Danish productions, is indeed named after choreographer August Bournonville.)

In 1717, the English impresario John Weaver had produced a ballet called *The Loves of Mars and Venus* entirely in mime at the Drury Lane Theatre in London. (This was long before those bestselling relationship advice books by John Gray.) Some say Sallé had seen that production as a young girl, which helped inspire her *Pygmalion*. Sounds good to me.

But anyway, it was Angiolini and Noverre who really developed the ballet d'action. Angiolini also created dances for Gluck's operas *Don Juan* and *Orfeo* (he did the nice Elysian Fields bits). He also travelled to St. Petersburg and Moscow, where he helped Catherine the Great establish the Russian ballet tradition that became so important later on. Angiolini's pupil Vincenzo Galeotti helped do much the same in Copenhagen for the Royal Danish Ballet.

Noverre did his bit to help Gluck, too. In particular, he rescued the premiere of Gluck's opera *Alceste* in Vienna in 1767. Noverre walked in on a rehearsal to find Gluck throwing his wig on the floor and stamping his feet in frustration because he couldn't get the chorus to move the way he wanted. Simple, said Noverre: Stick the singers in the wings and have a couple of real dancers on stage doing the movement. It worked like a charm, and has ever since. (This is in keeping with the general precept that singers should be heard but not seen.)

In 1754 Noverre created a Chinese-style ballet that delighted Paris and prompted the English producer David Garrick to bring it to Drury Lane. Bad timing, as it turned out. England and France were on the brink of the Seven Years' War, so tensions were high and London audiences weren't in the mood for anything French. Garrick tried to convince people that Noverre was actually Swiss (well, he was half-Swiss) but that didn't work. Even with King George III in the house, there were catcalls and hissing and booing from the audience and riots in the street, so Garrick had to cancel the run.

But all in all, Noverre had a successful career. He used to amuse Frederick the Great by doing imitations of various ballerinas, and he liked to tell dirty jokes to Voltaire. He created court ballets for King Louis XVI and Marie Antoinette — which was a pretty good gig until the French Revolution in 1789, when they got fired — and in 1778 he created choreography for Mozart's only ballet, *Les Petits Riens*. (When Mozart thanked him, he said it was nothing.)

In 1760 Noverre published his famous *Lettres en Dances et Ballets*, which is still a pretty good read today. And Noverre was a big one for helping to simplify dance costumes. He said dancers should get rid of bulky skirts, those ridiculous hooped panniers and tonnelets, shoes with heels and big buckles and anything else that got in the way of clear expression of physical movement.

Angiolini and Noverre both thought they were getting back closer to the ideals of the ancient Greeks and Romans. They had very little actual evidence to go on, but it sounded good to them. And who are we to argue? Noverre, by the way, was one of the few who was not impressed by the dancer Camargo. He said she was "neither pretty nor tall nor well formed" — which tended to put a crimp in things, for sure.

*Why ballet slippers
don't have rubber tips*

THE AGONY
OF DE-FEET

L ET'S FACE IT, when most people think of ballet — if they
think of ballet at all — they think of beautiful young
women dancing on tippytoes. That's what it's about, that's what
it's always been about, and that's all it's about.

Well, of course that's not true. But try telling most people that.

THE FACT IS THAT DANCING on point — or *en pointe*, to use the
fancy French term — is a relatively recent technique, and only
a very small part of what ballet is all about. It's an important part,
you bet, but still only a part nonetheless.[1]

Point work is barely 200 years old. That may seem like a long
time on the one hand (or the one foot), but considering ballet
has been around for more than 500 years, that's not even half the
time. And considering we've been dancing for, like, a million
years or so, it's hardly a drop in the bucket. Still, it *is* pretty
impressive to watch someone do it. Dancing on point takes
tremendous grace, skill, strength, balance and years of training
— not to mention a really good pair of shoes.[2]

NO ONE KNOWS FOR SURE who was the first dancer to dance on
her tiptoes. But the credit often goes to Marie Taglioni (1804-
84), who danced at the Paris Opéra but also over much of the
rest of Europe. She was born in Stockholm, where her father

---

[1] Certain breeds of hunting dogs will stand on point, but that's different.
[2] Don't try this at home, kids.

41

Philippe (or Filippo) Taglioni was a ballet master and her mother was the daughter of a leading opera singer. So it was what you'd call an artsy family.

Young Marie didn't take her first ballet lesson until she was nearly 12, by which time she and her mother and brothers were living in Paris while Daddy travelled around as a ballet master in Stockholm and Copenhagen and Vienna and Munich. To be truthful, her future didn't look very promising. She was skinny, stoop-shouldered and shy, having neither the posture nor the presence to be even a member of the *corps de ballet*, let alone a *prima ballerina*.

Of course, her father knew nothing of this, since Mommy had been sending him glowing letters about how talented their little darling was and how well her lessons were going and what a fabulous ballerina she was becoming. You know how mothers are.

When it came time for her to make her big dancing debut at 17, she wasn't at all ready. By this time the family was all together in Vienna, so her father began a rigorous training regimen that after only six months had her whipped into shape. (Well, not literally whipped, but he *was* pretty strict and demanding.) She made her real debut at the age of 18 in 1822 and wowed the crowds in Vienna, then Munich, and then Stuttgart. She no longer stooped, she'd filled out nicely, her technique was really quite good and she had the beginnings of that *je ne sais quoi* we call star power. Soon, she was to conquer the Paris Opéra as its *prima ballerina*.[3]

Among Taglioni's dancing partners in Stuttgart had been her brother Paul and the dancer Anton Stuhlmüller, who was later the lover of Fanny Elssler, the ballerina who became Marie Taglioni's main rival in Paris. Fanny Elssler had studied ballet as

---

[3] Her Paris career got off to a shaky start. For her second performance after her initial impressive debut, jealous dancers scattered the stage with bits of soap, hoping she would fall. Apparently, dancers do this kind of thing a lot.

a girl with Marie's father, and her own father had been a copyist and valet to Haydn. It's a small world, isn't it? (Being a valet seems to be a good way to get ahead in certain musical circles. Worked for Beaujoyeulx. Worked for Lully.)

Fanny Elssler often danced with her older sister Thérèse, who was very tall and would dress up as a man for such occasions. (People called her "the dancing giant.") Thérèse was also a good choreographer and the fact is that each of the Elssler girls was beautiful in her own way.[4]

Like Taglioni, Fanny Elssler also had Stuhlmüller as a dance partner, but that's not all they did together. Eventually they had a daughter and named her Theresa. Apart from Stuhlmüller, Elssler's other lovers over the years included King Ferdinand IV's son Prince Leopold, by whom she secretly had a son named Franz; the politician Friedrich von Gentz; the Marquis de la Valette, who'd already fathered children by two other dancers and wasn't really a marquis at all but only the illegitimate son of an actress and who made up the title as a way to pick up girls; and probably Henry Wikoff, a rich American who arranged for her debut in New York and a tour of the United States and Cuba.[5]

Her relationship with Wikoff ended badly, though. She accused him of stealing money and then it was all over. Rumor has it she was also lovers with the Count d'Orsay and the Earl of Chesterfield, but I can't swear to that. Rumor also has it that both she and her sister Thérèse were secretly the daughters of Haydn's boss, Prince Nicolaus Esterházy, but somehow I doubt it. In her later years Fanny Elssler apparently married Ferdinand of Saxe-Coburg-Gotha and so, for reasons too complicated to

---

[4] Reviewing Fanny's performance in *Le Diable boiteux*, writer and critic Théophile Gautier (who helped write the libretto for *Giselle*) spent a whole paragraph just on her legs.

[5] When Elssler got to Washington, the whole U.S. Congress adjourned just to go see her dance.

explain here, just missed out on becoming Queen of Spain.[6]

Marie Taglioni's love life was less active, and far less happy. She married a French count who turned out to be a worthless cad and who left her for urgent business in Constantinople after only a couple of months of marriage. But they were together long enough for her to become pregnant, a pregnancy that for a long time she tried to hide from the public, and even from her doctors, by saying she had a sore knee. For years afterward, "*mal au genou*" became a dancer's joking term for being pregnant.

ANYHOW, WE'RE STRAYING from the point here, which is the development of dancing *en pointe*. As I said, it's difficult if not impossible to pinpoint a date for the first point work, or to say who the dancer was. Dance historians and ballet fans argue over whether it was Geneviève Gosselin at the Paris Opéra or Amalia Brugnoli in Vienna or another Opéra dancer, Fanny Bias. But no matter, by the 1820s it had become an established technique.

Whoever may have done it first, it was certainly Marie Taglioni who perfected and popularized dancing *en pointe*. It was she, says historian Ivor Guest, who "raised *pointe* work from a feat to an art." Both feet, actually.[7]

This was especially true of her performance in March 1832 in *La Sylphide*. Philippe Taglioni provided the choreography for his daughter, and the music was by a French/German composer named Jean Madeleine Schneitzhoeffer. Neither the choreography nor the music from that production survives. The version

---

[6] Fanny Elssler was probably therefore somehow related by marriage to Albert of Saxe-Coburg-Gotha, the husband of England's Queen Victoria, but I'm not quite sure on the details there, and it hardly matters anyhow.

[7] At the height of her career, Marie Taglioni was so popular that some infatuated fans actually boiled a pair of her ballet slippers and ate them for dinner, as some sort of homage. Personally, I'd have sent her flowers and left it at that.

you might see danced today is from the Royal Danish Ballet in 1836, with choreography by August Bournonville and music by Herman Severin Løvenskjold.[8]

La Sylphide tells the story of a young Scotsman named James who's about to get married to a woman he's not sure he loves. (She's his cousin and her name's Effie, neither of which may have helped.) The night before their wedding, he falls asleep and dreams of a beautiful winged fairy, a sylphid or sylph, who flies down and tries to lure him away. He follows her into the forest, but thanks to an evil spell by the neighborhood wicked witch, her wings fall off and she dies. At the end of the ballet, some of her sister sylphs fly down to carry her away, leaving James alone in the woods while Effie goes off to marry someone else entirely. Bummer.[9]

With Marie Taglioni in the title role, in the flowing mid-length white dress designed by Eugène Lami that has come to be known as the Romantic tutu, dancing on tiptoe to appear appropriately light and fairy-like, and with fairies flying up and down from above on wires, *La Sylphide* was what you'd call a rousing success. It was also perfectly in keeping with the mood of the Romantic Movement that had Europe in thrall at this time. Fairies and sprites and sylphs and other magical creatures had become all the rage.[10]

DANCING *EN POINTE* is not something you can just learn to do overnight. It takes years of preparation and training. You know what they say: To do it properly, you've really got to keep on your toes.

---

[8] Poor old Schneitzhoeffer. The French mangled his name so badly he eventually printed up calling cards to read "Schneitzhoeffer (pronounced *Bertrand*)."

[9] By the way, don't confuse *La Sylphide* with *Les Sylphides*, a ballet to Chopin's piano music choreographed by Michel Fokine. That comes later.

[10] Some would argue there had always been fairies on stage in ballet, only now they were part of the plot.

And it can be very painful, which is why many professional ballet companies have a resident podiatrist or chiropodist on staff, or at least on call. It's also one of the few ballet moves that women, being generally smaller and lighter, can do much more easily than men. (*Les Ballets Trocadero* is a bunch of guys in drag dancing on tiptoe, but that's mostly a gimmick — granted, a very clever and amazingly skilful gimmick.)

The special *pointe* shoe started appearing in the 1860s. Before that, ballerinas would stuff the toes of their slippers with cotton or fabric, darn the tips to make them harder, and just hope for the best. Shoes with big, clunky heels had pretty much disappeared by the late 1700s, to be replaced by satin slippers, with long ribbons to tie them securely into place. The modern *pointe* shoe has a hard leather sole to give extra support, but no heel.[11]

The toe of a point shoe has several layers of canvas or fabric shaped into a box and glued together with resin. As you wear them, your body heat softens the resin until the box eventually breaks down and dancing on them becomes, well, pointless. Dancers will sometimes wear out more than one pair of point shoes during a really strenuous performance. In Tchaikovsky's *Swan Lake*, the *prima ballerina* needs two different pairs, one as the Swan Queen and one as the Black Swan.

Ballerinas have sometimes tried other material for the toe box, but generally they've found that fabric works best. Steel-toed shoes may be useful in some other professions — construction or police work, for instance — but for a ballerina they make way too much noise, unless you want to be tap dancing. (The Rockettes at Radio City Music Hall in New York did some tap dancing *en pointe* in the 1960s and '70s. Or some I'm told. I wasn't there.)

---

[11] There were still plenty of heels on the stage, but just none on the shoes.

And obviously, rubber tips run the risk of being too bouncy and sending you flying off into the wings or into the pit.[12]

FOR CERTAIN ROLES or specialty numbers, male or female dancers sometimes wear "character boots," which are regular dancing shoes disguised to look like something else. For instance, there's a lot of heel clicking in *Coppélia* and in Jean Dauberval's *La Fille Mal Gardée*, the Widow Simone dances a clog dance in wooden shoes that are traditionally bright yellow. And I guess if anyone ever choreographed a ballet to the music of Elvis Presley, the dancers would all be wearing blue suede shoes.

---

[12] Shoes with a rubber sole might be appropriate for a Beatles ballet.

Giselle getting the willies

ROTTEN TO
THE CORPS

A S THE ROMANTIC MOVEMENT swept across Europe, in much the same way as the minuet had done before (see joke in Chapter 4), it was to have a major impact on the development of ballet. Several major impacts, actually.

As storytelling became more elaborate and fantastic, so did the theatres in which the stories were told. There had long been elaborate stage devices, from the days of Leonardo da Vinci's gimmicks through to that erupting volcano in *Les Indes Galantes* in 1735. But now, with flying backdrops (not to mention flying sylphids) and curtains out front and in the wings, and with other devices, theatre stages began more to resemble the "proscenium arch" or "picture frame" (or, if you want to be modern, "TV tube" or "computer screen") design of today.

The use of wax candles for lighting had begun to wane, to be replaced by those new-fangled gaslamps. (Back in the days of Lully and Molière, the lighting was so bad that audience members often brought their own candles — which at least made it easier to wax rhapsodic over a wonderful performance.)[1]

There were also big social changes afoot, and not just in ballet. The French Revolution in (where else?) France, and the Industrial Revolution in England and elsewhere in Europe, had led to the rise of a richer middle class. New ideas were taking

---

[1] It took 10,000 candles to light Louis XIV's theatre at Versailles. He didn't use it much – all that lighting and blowing out got to be too much trouble, even if you have servants to do all the work for you.

shape, old notions being discarded. No longer were ballets and operas and plays and concerts the exclusive domain of a privileged few aristocrats. Now plain, ordinary folks could go and be bored by them too. Or, as music historian Ivor Guest so eloquently puts it: "A new wealthy class, which had grown rich through the expansion of industry and commerce, was taking its place in society, and people were beginning to view many problems in a different light."[2]

Romanticism, with its emphasis on love, death, anger, passion and other strong emotions, became the dominant mode of artistic expression in the 19th century, whether in ballet or opera or symphonies or the visual arts. (For the Romantics, as one writer says, "Passion was king, as Reason once had been, and the Irrational was worshipped as a God." Just think of Romanticism as one big, awkward, adolescent kid. You get the picture.)[3]

The Romantics were also big on supernatural elements, whether the dancing fairies of *La Sylphide* or something a little darker. As for instance in *Robert le Diable* (*Robert the Devil*), a grand opera by Giacomo Meyerbeer (1791-1864) first performed at the Paris Opéra in 1831. (At this time, although ballet existed as a separate art form, it was still also often an integral part of opera performances, especially for the French. The Italians were beginning to prefer their opera straight up, with a little ballet on the side.) Once again, Philippe Taglioni choreographed his daughter Marie for the major ballet sequences.

And they were humdingers. In Act III, set in the moonlit ruins of an old cloister, the spirits of a bunch of dead, defrocked nuns who'd broken all their vows dance a sexy, seductive dance to lure the hero, Robert, into doing something diabolical. Marie

---

[2] See reference to gaslamps, above.

[3] Speaking of big, awkward adolescents, somewhere along the way we've forgotten to mention *The Creatures of Prometheus*, a ballet by that seminal Romantic composer, Ludwig van Beethoven. It's the only one he wrote and he finished it in 1801 for the Italian choreographer Salvatore Viganò. Viganò was Boccherini's nephew, by the way.

Taglioni danced the role of the abbess, the head nun, an ethere-al, wicked beauty. The crowds went wild.[4]

The opening night of *Robert le Diable* was one of those big theatrical disasters that producers and actors live in terror of and audiences find especially entertaining. One of the ballerinas, Julie-Aimée Dorus, nearly got beaned by a falling gaslamp. In Act III, Taglioni herself had to jump out of the way to avoid a bit of scenery crashing down, and the principal tenor, Adolphe Nourrit, accidentally fell through a trapdoor. It was just one of those nights.

Despite the name Giacomo, by the way, Meyerbeer wasn't Italian at all (and he added the Meyer later). He was a German from Berlin named Jakob Beer. The libretto for *Robert le Diable* was, appropriately enough, written by a man named Scribe.

SUPERNATURAL CREATURES SHOW UP again in another popular Romantic ballet, *Giselle*, first performed in 1841, with music by Adolphe Adam and choreography by Jean Coralli and Jules Perrot. Perrot, himself a very fine Romantic dancer, was the lover of the ballerina in the title role, Carlotta Grisi — not that it's anyone else's business, really. Adam's other claim to fame is as the composer of the Christmas hymn we know as *O Holy Night*. I don't know who his lovers were, or even if he had any. None of our business, either.

Giselle tells the story of a peasant girl who finds out her boyfriend is already engaged to another woman, which general-ly would come as a bit of a shock. She takes the news rather badly. In fact, she goes mad with grief and dies, coming back in Act II as a sort of vampire, or *wili*, with a bunch of other disaffected vampire women. The French subtitle is *Les Wilis*, and the ballet can sometimes give you the willies. You might consider them the original phantoms of the Opéra.

---

[4] Nowadays it would be a TV special: *When Nuns Go Bad*

Speaking of women, it's become fashionable in certain circles to debate whether *La Révolte des femmes* (*The Revolt of the Women*), sometimes known as *La Révolte au Sérail* (*The Revolt at the Harem*), which was a Taglioni team event in 1833, the year after *Les Sylphides*, is an important proto-feminist ballet or just another example of cheap, sexist exploitation. We haven't time for that now.

For quite a different production in London in 1845 for the producer Benjamin Lumley, Perrot was asked to choreograph an unprecedented *Pas de Quatre* featuring four of the most famous ballerinas of the day — Marie Taglioni, Carlotta Grisi, Fanny Cerrito and Lucile Grahn. As you can imagine, the potential for clashing egos and bitchy rivalry was great. The other three ballerinas had graciously agreed that the final solo, the place of honor, should go to Taglioni. But they were fighting over who else should get to dance last, just before her. Lumley solved the problem by telling Perrot the dancers would appear by order of their ages, with the oldest one dancing last. For some reason, they all stopped fighting after that. How's *that* for crisis management?

AMONG THE MOST PROMISING of the Romantic ballerinas was also, sadly, ill-fated. She danced as Emma Livry, though that was only a stage name. Her mother, Célestine Emarot, was at the Opéra, but seemed to have more success as a lover than as a dancer, especially after she hooked up with Baron Charles de Chassiron and had Emma a little while after that.

In 1858, Emma Livry (Emma Emarot must have sounded too awkward) made her debut in the title role of *La Sylphide* and was so impressive she lured the great Marie Taglioni out of retirement and to see her, and later to coach her. Other roles followed, by which her reputation for grace, charm and artistry increased — and so did her salary. Emma Livry was slender and graceful, but truth be told, she was no great beauty. Even her champions had to admit that her nose was too big and her chin

Emma Livry plays it cool

too small, which made her a great target for cartoon caricaturists of the day. But she had lovely eyes.

In 1860, Taglioni herself created a new ballet for Livry, *Le Papillon* (*The Butterfly*), to music by Jacques Offenbach. But alas, Livry's success was to be short-lived. Despite dire warnings of the dangers of fire (again with the gaslamps!), Emma Livry refused to follow the practice enforced by management of dipping her costume in a special fire-retardant liquid. She thought it made her dress look limp and dingy.

Then one day in 1862, rehearsing a revival of *La Muette de Portici*, Livry got too close to a light and her dress burst into flame. She died eight months later from the burns. That's what you get for ignoring your contract. At least for another dancer, the end had come sooner. In 1844, Clara Webster's dress caught fire and she died only three days later. Who'd have thought ballet would be considered a life-threatening occupation?[5]

ANOTHER HUGELY POPULAR ballet from this period, which has stayed in the repertoire ever since, is *Coppélia*, with music by Léo Delibes and choreography by Arthur Saint-Léon. Like other Romantic ballets, it has magical elements, though it's not nearly so morbid as *La Sylphide* or *Giselle*. For one thing, nobody dies.[6]

Based on a tale by the German writer E.T.A. Hoffmann, *Coppélia* is a sort of *Pinocchio* ripoff and tells the story of two lovers, Frantz and Swanilda, an old toymaker named Coppelius and his daughter Coppelia, who's really a toy doll he's trying to bring magically to life. As a title, *Coppélia* is considered less awkward than its alternative, *La Fille aux Yeux d'Email* (*The Girl With*

---

[5] Writers at the time and since have made many Romantic allusions to Livry as *le papillon*, the butterfly or moth drawn inexorably and tragically to the flame. I've decided not to, myself. Too obvious.

[6] Saint-Léon was the husband of the ballerina Fanny Cerrito, in case you're keeping track of these things.

the Enamel Eyes) Somehow that doesn't seem like much of a compliment.

The ballet opens with Frantz falling in love with the doll he sees reading a book in the window, because he thinks she's real. (Frantz is not the sharpest knife in the drawer, if you know what I mean.) This of course makes Swanilda jealous, never a good thing. But after she breaks into the toyshop and finds out Coppelia is only a doll, Swanilda decides to play a trick on the toymaker and her boyfriend by dressing up in her costume, so when he does his magical incantations and brings her to life, it's really just Swanilda in disguise. Are you following this?[7]

Anyhow, it all ends happily, more or less, with Frantz and Swanilda making up and getting married. (Well, most people still consider that to be a happy ending).[8]

Coppélia was a big success from its debut, though it got off to a rocky start. The librettist, Charles Nuitter, wanted the young ballerina Léontine Beaugard in the title role, but the theatre management decided to go with a "name," and imported the Russian ballerina Adèle Grantsova instead. But after rehearsals dragged on too long, Grantsova went home and the role went to a young Italian, Giuseppina Bozzacchi. She premiered the role in 1870, but then the Franco-Prussian War broke out and she died of a fever from smallpox on her 17th birthday, which hardly seems fair. (Saint-Léon himself, not long after, died of exhaustion. But at least it wasn't his birthday.) Beaugard got her chance at the role for a revival in 1871 and she was a big success.

Delibes wrote another ballet, called *Sylvia*, as well as the opera *Lakmé* and a bunch of other assorted music. He was much

---

[7] And don't confuse Swanilda with Brünnhilde, the tin-plated Valkyrie in Wagner's operas. That would be an even bigger mistake.

[8] If there isn't one already, I'm sure there's a porno version of *Coppélia* to be made, with that full-grown doll coming to life and everything. We'd better not go there.

admired by Tchaikovsky, who liked his music more than that of Brahms. (Not to put too fine a point on it, Tchaikovsky thought Brahms was a "giftless bastard.") In a letter to his patron, Tchaikovsky wrote, "My own *Swan Lake* is simply trash in comparison with *Sylvia*." Well, I wouldn't go *that* far.

A LOT OF SCHOLARS will tell you French ballet went into a bit of a decline at the end of the 19th century, and who are we to argue? Oh sure, it was still beautiful and graceful, and there were lots of lovely ballerinas — just look at any of those famous Degas paintings from the period and you'll see them.

But artistically, it was not what you could call a high point in the development of ballet. The emphasis on the star ballerina tended to shove the regular chorus dancers way into the background, which was pretty rotten to the *corps*. But even at that, although there were some very capable prima ballerinas dancing in Paris — the Italian Carlotta Zambelli, the Danish Adeline Genée, for instance — none of them could match the innovations or accomplishments of a Taglioni or an Elssler or a Camargo or a Sallé.

FINDING SERIOUS BALLET WORK at this time got so difficult, in fact, that Genée spent most of her later career doing song-and-dance routines for boisterous, drunken crowds in English music halls. (As early as the 1850s, lamenting the decline of ballet as a serious art form, the English ballet producer Benjamin Lumley had complained that audiences "only want legs, not brains.")

Speaking of Taglioni and innovation — and legs — she is often credited with having invented legwarmers. The story goes she got cold during a particularly rigorous training session, so she cut the sleeves off a sweater and put them on her legs.

This wasn't just a trendy fashion statement, it was pure practicality. Dancers know if they cool down too quickly, their muscles might seize up.

AND IT WAS CERTAINLY NOT a great time for male ballet dancers. Although men had dominated the stage in the early decades of ballet, by this time they were relegated mostly to mere supporting roles. (Literally supporting — they were there mostly just to lift the ballerinas up in the air.) It had gotten so bad that at its premiere in 1870, even the male lead role of Frantz in *Coppélia* was danced not by a man but by a ballerina, Eugénie Fiocre, who apparently looked quite dishy in drag (if you like that sort of thing, and I know many of you do). That tradition, of having a woman dance as Frantz, continued in Paris until the mid-1950s. No wonder so many dancers are confused about their sexuality.

Over in Italy, meanwhile, the choreographer Luigi Manzotti was going in for big, lavish, ridiculous spectacles that, while impressive, didn't have much in the way of plot or character or emotional insight. (A lot like today's big Hollywood blockbuster special-effects films, come to think of it.) His ballet *Amor* calls for more than 500 dancers, 18 horses, two elephants and an ox. From this we can conclude two things:

1. Stravinsky wasn't the first one after all to write a ballet for elephants,

and

2. Manzotti's budget must have run out before he got to the partridge in a pear tree.

Making a splash with Swan Lake

Swanning Around and Cracking Nuts

B ALLET IN FRANCE was losing its footing at the end of the 19th century, but all was not lost. Over in Russia, important steps were being taken, and then the composer Tchaikovsky jumped in to save the day.

IT'S A WONDER TCHAIKOVSKY found time to write any ballets at all, really, what with everything else he had on his plate. He composed all those symphonies, for one thing (six altogether, although that last one was pretty pathetic), not to mention about eight operas, the "fantasy overture" *Romeo and Juliet* (which had started out to be a ballet but never quite made it), the *1812 Overture*, a few piano concertos and a whole slew of smaller bits of music here and there.

And then there was his private life — which was, let's face it, a mess.

During some of this time he even managed to hold down a real job — if you can call working for the government a real job. Nevertheless, he somehow found the time to compose music for three of the most important, or at least certainly the most popular, ballets in the repertoire — *Swan Lake, Sleeping Beauty* and *The Nutcracker*. Not only did these help revive ballet in the second half of the 19th century, they were a good thing for Russian music in general.[1]

---

[1] Though that's not what the Mighty Five had to say on the subject. They thought Tchaikovsky wasn't nearly Russian enough. He, meanwhile, thought

FOR A LONG TIME, Russian culture — music, dancing, even the way they dress — had pretty much kept to itself, avoiding outside influences. It helped that Russians spoke a different language and used a different alphabet, with R's that look like P's and some letters that look like nothing else you've ever seen.[2]

Christianity had made its way in by the 10th century, but even then it took on a peculiarly Russian flavor. In 1636 Joseph, the patriarch of the Russian Orthodox Church, outlawed all music-making in the home, which was unsporting, culturally speaking. He changed his mind later on, but some people never really got over it.

Russian folkdancing up to this point seemed to consist largely of people kicking out their legs, shouting a lot and throwing big knives into the floor. It's impressive as heck, but it's kind of hard on the flooring. And there's always the risk of stabbing your dancers in the tootsies, which they tend to resent.

IN THE 17TH CENTURY, Czar Peter the Great did much to bring Western customs, including Western music, to Russia. One of his brainwaves was forcing the *boyars*, or old fuddy-duddies, to shave off their long beards and cut back their long robes — which certainly made dancing easier, for one thing. Later on, he decided they could keep their beards after all, but only if they paid a special tax, and only if they carried around a licence to prove they'd paid up.[3]

Peter's daughter, Empress Elizabeth, had an opera house built, but she often had a hard time persuading the noblemen and ladies in her court to go to the performances. Pretty soon she found that if threats weren't effective, a bribe or two generally

---

they were a bunch of old farts. It's quite an interesting debate, but don't get me started.

[2] Tell Russians to mind their P's and Q's and they'll just look at you blankly.

[3] A beard licence is not the same as poetic licence, which is more the kind of thing I'm doing right now.

worked wonders. And in those days, of course, where there was opera there was generally also ballet (just to remind you we're keeping on track).

All of these cultural goings-on, by the way, were going on in a brand new city Peter had dreamt up to replace Moscow as the capital. He got thousands of peasants to build it for him out in the middle of nowhere in a swampy spot at the edge of the Baltic Sea. And naturally he named it St. Petersburg, after himself — modesty not being one of his strong suits.[4]

St. Petersburg was later renamed Petrograd and then Leningrad for a while under the Soviets, but now it's St. Petersburg again, even though the capital got moved back to Moscow somewhere along the way and has stayed there since.

Anyway, it was another Great, the empress Catherine the Great, in the 18th century, who really did a lot to help ballet and opera flourish in Russia. She was the one, you'll recall if you review your notes from Chapter 5, who invited ballet master Gaspero Angiolini to bring his *ballet d'action* productions in the 1760s. She also invited all sorts of famous opera composers — Salieri, Paisiello, Cimarosa and others — to premiere their works in St. Petersburg. They were happy to come, so long as Catherine was footing the bills. Unlike Peter, Catherine seems wisely to have avoided the temptation of renaming the city after herself — St. Catherinesburg or whatever. She knew her limits.

Catherine, interestingly enough, wasn't even Russian and her name wasn't originally Catherine. She'd started out as a little German girl named Princess Sophia Augusta Frederica of Anhalt-Zerbst. How she grew up to become Imperial Empress of all Russia is a fascinating story of girlhood determination and pluck, but it's way too complicated to get into it now. Let's just say she married well.[5]

---

4 It's hard to be modest when you're nearly 6 feet 9 inches tall and in charge of a huge, sprawling empire.

5 There were even rumors Catherine was the illegitimate daughter of

By the time Tchaikovsky came along in the 19th century, Russia had established an enviable reputation for ballet performance, both in St. Petersburg at the Maryinsky Theatre and, to a lesser degree, at the Bolshoi Theatre in Moscow. It was the Bolshoi that commissioned him to write a new ballet, based on a German legend and to be called *Swan Lake*. Never having written a ballet and keen to try his hand at a new form of expression, Tchaikovsky eagerly accepted. Besides, he needed the money.

Tchaikovsky was born in the small Russian town of Kamsko-Votkinsk, a provincial backwater where not a lot went on, culturally speaking. It wasn't exactly Siberia, but you were about halfway there. Tchaikovsky's father, Ilya Petrovich Tchaikovsky, was a mining engineer who worked hard and tried his best and only wanted his son to get a good job. Ilya's father, Pyotr Fyodorovich Tchaikovsky, had been chief of police in a nearby region and did a little faith-healing on the side.[6]

Tchaikovsky's mother, Alexandra d'Assier, was Ilya's second wife and the daughter of a French noble family that had fled to Russia after Louis XIV revoked the Edict of Nantes back in 1685.[7]

They had a little boy in 1840 and named him Pyotr Ilyich. Translating from Russian is always a bit tricky (there's that funny alphabet, for one thing) and his first name is sometimes spelt Piotr, but it's usually anglicized as Peter. (In the family, his pet name was "Petya.") Sometimes the Ilyich is given as Ilych, but that might just be a typo. Lately, of course, there's been a

---

Frederick the Great of Prussia, but I find this highly unlikely. Frederick wasn't interested in that sort of activity.

[6] Handy to have a faith-healer in the family, I always say. As part of his job as mining inspector, Tchaikovsky's father had his own private army of a hundred Cossacks. I wouldn't know what to do with them, myself.

[7] You see how everything's connected? If you don't remember the Edict of Nantes, go back and review Chapter 3. It may be on the exam.

move — chiefly among transliteral pedants, demented librarians and other smartypants knowitalls — to spell his surname Chaikovsky, or even Chaikovski. Just ignore them and maybe they'll go away.

Little Pyotr, or Piotr, or Peter, or Petya, was a shy, sensitive child who cried a lot. If you were lucky, you could eventually calm him down till it was maybe a whimper. Scholars have noted that his nanny (whose name was Fanny, by the way) once called him "a porcelain child." Actually, there's another one of those scholarly debates there. It seems what she actually called him was *un enfant du verre*," or "a child of glass." But somehow, the "porcelain" remark has stuck around, being quoted again and again. Not knowing any better at the time, even I refer to it in my earlier book *Bach, Beethoven and the Boys*. I'm happy now to be able to set the record straight (and cleverly to get in a plug for my earlier work). Even as a grown man, Tchaikovsky remained the weepy, emotional type. His music's that way, too.[8]

What made Tchaikovsky so weepy? Some of the usual reasons — for one thing, he was a Romantic, and for another, he was a struggling, underappreciated composer who was nearly always broke. (To make ends meet, he sometimes had to borrow money from his servant, Alexey. This is not done in the best circles.) For the first part of his life he had a boring, unfulfilling job as a law clerk at the Ministry of Justice, though he was later able to quit that and take a job (even if it meant less money) teaching harmony at the Moscow Conservatory of Music.

But even when he was able to devote more time to composing it was an uphill battle. The critics hated his music and the Mighty Five thought it should sound more Russian (that is, more like *their's*). Anton Rubenstein, under whom the young composer had studied at the St. Petersburg Conservatory, considered Tchaikovsky's first piano concerto (*No. 1 in B-flat*, 1874)

---

[8] Arriving at a New York hotel for an American tour in 1891, Tchaikovsky writes in a letter, "I made myself at home. First of all, I wept rather long."

63

"unplayable." Amazingly, everybody started playing it anyway and even Rubenstein himself grudgingly had to learn to play it eventually.

PROFESSIONALLY, THINGS KEPT getting better and better for Tchaikovsky. Rubenstein and the Five notwithstanding, his works were gaining greater acceptance, and in 1877 he found a steady source of income from Nadedja von Meck, a wealthy widow and socialite with more money than she knew what to do with. (With 11 children of her own, you'd think she'd have more than enough places to spend it, but apparently not.) Von Meck kind of adopted Tchaikovsky as her own pet composer, though oddly enough she insisted they never meet — which, aside from one accidental encounter in the street one day, they never did. (When he died she sent a wreath, but no card. By then they'd had a bit of a falling out.)

But at the same time, Tchaikovsky's personal life just kept getting worse and worse — which would account for much of the weepiness. As a young man he became infatuated with a pretty young French soprano named Desirée Artot, but she went off and married someone else — which was just as well, as it turns out. (Inspired by this quasi-romance, he wrote the *Romeo and Juliet* overture, so at least something good came out of it.)

Then a young woman student at the Moscow Conservatory named Antonina Miliukova latched on and persuaded him to marry her, which was a big mistake. He was secretly a homosexual and she was openly a nymphomaniac who thought she could "reform" him — and you know that hardly *ever* works. He may have wanted to come out of the closet, but all she wanted to do was go into the bedroom. All around, it was not a good combination. ("Physically," he wrote in a letter to his brother, Modest, "she is totally repulsive to me." That should have been a clue right there.)

So he tried to kill himself, the marriage broke up, she wound up in an asylum — it was a big mess. Not a good scene, except if you're looking for material for an afternoon soap opera.

BUT ON THE BALLET FRONT, things were looking much better, relatively speaking. The Moscow Bolshoi had commissioned *Swan Lake* in 1894 and it had its premiere performance in a shortened version that year.

THE STORY, SET IN MEDIEVAL GERMANY, tells of handsome prince looking for a wife. One day out hunting, he finds a lake with a bunch of swans (hence the title), who turn out to be beautiful women under a magic spell of an evil magician disguised as a big owl. The prince's name, by the way, is Siegfried — but don't confuse him with Wagner's Siegfried. Different guy.[9]

Siegfried meets Odette, a white swan who's the Swan Queen, and they fall instantly in love. (As a swan, he figures she'll be good at necking.) He even promises to marry her if she'll come to a fancy costume ball at his castle. This gives the choreographer a cheesy excuse for scenes with a bunch of character dancing in colorful native costumes. Odette says she can't come while still under the evil spell, which will be broken if Siegfried keeps his promise of love to her.

That night at the ball, the evil magician, Rotbart, arrives with his daughter Odile, a Black Swan whom he has magically caused to look just like Odette. (Still with me?) Siegfried, of course, who hasn't read ahead in the program, falls in love with the wrong girl, particularly because as the Black Swan she dances 32 *fouettés* in a row, which impresses him no end. (He's thinking, 'Forget the necking. If she can do *that* ...')

But because Siegfried has betrayed his love to Odette, that means nasty old Rotbart wins and the spell is binding and remains in full force, hereinafter and heretofore and notwithstanding, as described in section 2, paragraph 3, subsection B,

---

[9] For a composer who wrote no ballets whatsoever, Wagner seems to crop up a lot anyway. Annoying, isn't it?

clause *iv*. The original version of the story ends tragically, with Siegfried rushing to the lake to look for Odette and being killed by Rotbart, thus leaving Odette sad and lonely and doomed forever to be a swan.

In some versions there's a happy ending, where Siegfried rushes to the lake and apologizes to Odette, grovelling all about Rotbart and the whole Odette/Odile thing. ("Honest, honeybunch, I thought she was *you!*") After being huffy for awhile, Odette forgives him and they dance a lovely *pas de deux*. Then Rotbart comes in, all mad, and tries to flood the lake and drown them all. But he's neglected to fill out the requisite environmental-impact forms and Siegfried declares his willingness to die for Odette, which breaks the spell. The lake subsides and the swans all become women again.

THE BOLSHOI PREMIERE OF *SWAN LAKE* didn't go particularly well, notes Tchaikovsky biographer Anthony Holden, "thanks to the inadequacy of the choreographer, conductor, dancers and orchestra." That covers pretty much everybody, I guess, except the composer.

It certainly wasn't Tchaikovsky's fault. The conductor, some guy named Ryabov, was a rank amateur who barely knew what he was doing. (Not that Tchaikovsky would have done any better. Whenever he conducted, he had this morbid fear his head would fall off, so he'd hold onto it with his left hand and try to conduct with only his right.) And the leading role of Odette, the White Swan, should have gone to the company's *prima ballerina*, Anna Sobeshchanskaya, but for the first few nights it went instead to her less talented rival, Pelagaya Karpakova. Maybe Sobeshchanskaya's name was too long to fit on the program, or maybe it had something to do with all that money being thrown around by Karpakova's rich husband, a Greek millionaire.[10]

---

[10] Greek millionaires are always handy to have around. Just ask Maria Callas.

And as if all that weren't bad enough, the critics hated it because the original story was German and so therefore — you guessed it — not Russian enough. (Ironically, the Viennese critic Eduard Hanslick once slammed *Romeo and Juliet* as "*etwas zu russisch*," or "decidedly too Russian." You just can't win sometimes.)

BUT THINGS WENT MUCH BETTER later, when Marius Petipa, a French choreographer who'd come to St. Petersburg as a dancer in 1847, got hold of *Swan Lake* in 1895 and rechoreographed it into the version we might see today. In the original production, Odette and Odile were two different dancers, but it was Petipa's brainwave to have the same ballerina dance both roles — making the whole Odette/Odile mistaken-identity thing a whole lot more convincing (although it does make it a tough slog for the poor ballerina).

It was the Italian ballerina Pierina Legnani who first danced the dual Odette/Odile role for Petipa, and it was she who first created the now-famous 32 *fouettés* (not to mention 32 *échappés* in another part of the story). No wonder ballerinas in this role often go through several pairs of *pointe* shoes, both black and white. Since then, the role has gone on to become a *tour de force* to display the talent of a long line of Russian *prima ballerinas*, including Anna Pavlova and Olga Preobrazhenskaya. (Alicia Markova, also famous for the role, wasn't Russian at all. She'd started out as plain old Alice Marks.)[11]

Nijinsky was one of many famous Siegfrieds, but it's not nearly as impressive a role for the male dancer. All he does most of the time is prop up swans.

---

[11] The Russians do love their ballerinas. After Czar Paul I took over from Catherine the Great in 1796, he fired the male dancers at the Bolshoi and replaced them all with ballerinas in drag. He would have loved Marlene Dietrich.

IRONICALLY, ALTHOUGH IT'S GONE ON to become one of his most famous and best-loved works, Tchaikovsky never thought much of *Swan Lake* and never lived to see a full production of it. After the disastrous premiere, which wasn't the whole thing anyway, all he saw were bits and pieces. At least he was spared having to suffer through any of those ludicrous happy endings tacked on later, and which he would have hated. He liked his love affairs tragic or unrequited.[12]

Choreographer Matthew Bourne caused a stir recently with his updated reinterpretation of the ballet, which premiered in London in 1996 and which many people consider a "gay" version of the story. (The hero has a girlfriend, but all the swans — including the Black Swan — are male). Tchaikovsky would have loved it.

TCHAIKOVSKY TEAMED UP with Petipa again for his next ballet, *Sleeping Beauty*, based on the classic fairy tale, which he started writing in 1888 and which had its premiere at the Maryinsky Theatre in St. Petersburg in 1890. Tsar Nicholas II himself went to the dress rehearsal, though evidently he didn't know much about music, or ballet. When asked what he thought of the performance, all he could manage was, "Very nice." He was a man of few words.

Considering his affection, and affinity, for classic fairy tales, it's both a surprise and a pity that Tchaikovsky never wrote a ballet on the story of *Cinderella*. Maybe he couldn't figure out how to manage the dancing in those glass slippers. Too dangerous.

It took another Russian composer of a later generation, Sergei Prokofiev, to create a *Cinderella* ballet, which he did in

---

[12] For many years, Tchaikovsky had a mad crush on his young nephew, Vladimir Davidov, known in the family as "Bob," who was the inspiration for his *Sixth Symphony*, the *Pathétique*. And in the end, the composer killed himself to avoid scandal over an infatuation with the 18-year-old nephew of a prominent nobleman. His name, if you must know, was Alexander Vladimirovich Stenbok-Fermor.

Pytor Ilyich was one cracked nut

1944. (Prokofiev also created another ballet Tchaikovsky never completed, a full version of *Romeo and Juliet*. He probably didn't waste so much of his time crying.)

WITHOUT QUESTION THE BEST-KNOWN and most popular of Tchaikovsky's ballets was his third and last, *The Nutcracker*. Ironic, really, since it was one he didn't particularly want to write. Ivan Vsevolozhsky, the director of the Imperial Theatres and the same guy who'd commissioned *Sleeping Beauty*, wanted a new ballet. But Tchaikovsky was more interested in writing a new opera, *Iolanta*. It ended up being a package deal — Tchaikovsky agreed to write the new ballet only as part of a double bill with the new opera. He thought the opera was going to be a huge success, but he was wrong there. Gilbert and Sullivan had much better luck with their operetta *Iolanthe*. Similar title — totally different story.

It took Tchaikovsky only about a month or so to sketch the music for *The Nutcracker* in June 1892, but he dawdled for many months after that over the orchestration. The plot comes from the story *Nussknacker und Mausekönig* (*The Nutcracker and the Mouse-King*) by E.T.A. Hoffmann, who you'll remember also provided the story for *Coppélia*.

Tchaikovsky didn't like it much — thought it was too silly and, for a children's story, didn't actually give the children much to do — but he nevertheless wrote some wonderful music for it. What a trouper. In Russian, by the way, the ballet is called *Shchelkunchik*, but it's now know almost everywhere by its English title. Except in France, people who call it *Casse-noisette* are usually just being pretentious.

The Tsar came to its dress rehearsal too, and this time he positively gushed over how much he liked it. But at the premiere the press didn't agree. One review complained it was "completely devoid of creativity." Like, mice duking it out with toy soldiers isn't creative? Critics! What are you gonna do? Since then *The Nutcracker*, with its dancing goldfish and flowers and sugar-plum fairies, has become a perennial favorite — as much a part of Christmas tradition for many people as Santa and nativity scenes and end-of-the-year clearance sales.

The Nutcracker has become a perennial favorite the world over and ballet companies everywhere, large and small, mount productions every year, much in the same way that choirs revive Handel's *Messiah*, though with considerably more creative interpretation. My own favorite *Nutcracker* production features the usual doddering uncle turned into an Amelia Earhart-like aunt, who makes her first flamboyant entrance wearing pilot's goggles and rollerskates. Now, *there's* something I'd like to see — a *Messiah* on rollerskates![13]

---

[13] The Russian playwright Anton Chekov takes much of the charm out of ballet with this candid remark: "I don't understand anything at all about the ballet. All I know is that during the intervals the ballerinas stink like horses." I wonder what the horses think of that?

Nijinsky blending into the fauna

SACRE BLEU!

B Y THE END OF THE 19TH CENTURY, Tchaikovsky had helped raise ballet to such a creative and expressive pinnacle you could say it was standing on its tippytoes, artistically speaking. But it took another Russian composer to shake it up and make sure it didn't get boring. Those Russians — always up to something!

Igor Fedorovich Stravinsky (1882-1971) was born in the Russian town of Oranienbaum and grew up in St. Petersburg (it still hadn't become Petrograd yet, let alone Leningrad), although the family liked to spend summers out in the country when they could. Sometimes they found a relative to sponge off for a while, which was even better. (Stravinsky's mother's brother-in-law had a big estate in Volhynia that was quite nice.)

Stravinsky's father was a musician, a bass-baritone at the Imperial Opera, and music lessons in piano and harmony and counterpoint were all part of his growing up. But then the father sent his son to St. Petersburg University to study law. Maybe he thought one starving artist in the family was enough.[1]

But you know how it is: Tell kids they mustn't do something and that's exactly what they'll do. By the time he was 20, Stravinsky was determined to become a great composer. Maybe that was all secretly part of his father's plan. Who

---

[1] Music history is filled with composers whose parents wanted them to become lawyers — Handel, Schumann, Tchaikovsky, Elgar, to name a few. Ralph Vaughan Williams came from a long line of lawyers on his father's side. On his mother's side they made plates — she was a Wedgwood.

knows? Anyway, Stravinsky sought the advice of the great Russian composer Rimsky-Korsakov, who said, in effect, "Kid, don't quit your day job," but agreed to take the young man on as a private pupil.

Rimsky-Korsakov taught Stravinsky for six years, and when he died in 1908 Stravinsky composed a lovely funeral piece in his honor. At least, I assume it was lovely but I can't say for sure. Someone misplaced it during that little revolution the Russians had back then.[2]

A little before then, in 1906, Stravinsky had married Catherine Nossenko, who was his first cousin, and they went on to have four kids — two girls and two boys. Evidently, Stravinsky worried more about symmetry in his personal life than in his musical rhythms, which are more often uneven.[3]

IT WAS IN 1908 THAT STRAVINSKY first encountered Serge Diaghilev, who was to have such a big impact on the ballet scene of the early 20th century. Diaghilev wasn't himself a composer, or even much of a writer, though he helped run an arts magazine for a while. And although he loved art, he couldn't paint worth beans. But he was artistic and creative in the broadest sense. His artistry lay in being able to conceive great ideas, and then in finding the right artists to help realize them. (But don't call him an entrepreneur — he hated that term.)

A great part of what made the *Ballets Russes* so remarkable and wonderful, in fact, was Diaghilev's very gift for bringing artists together. As well as Stravinsky, the company featured works by such composers as Prokofiev, Ravel, Satie and Poulenc. Picasso, Matisse and Miró were among the artists who

---

[2] Oh, you know the one. It was in all the papers.

[3] Music history is also filled with composers who married their cousins — Milhaud, Webern, Rachmaninov, Stravinsky, Grieg, Meyerbeer, J.S. Bach. I'm not sure what this means, if it means anything at all. Maybe it's better not to think about it. The adjective relating to cousins, by the way, is "consorbrinal," but you hardly ever hear it come up in conversation.

created set designs, and Jean Cocteau provided stories. As well as Fokine, Diaghilev's choreographers included Nijinsky himself and George Balanchine, who later left for America and established the New York City Ballet, which has had an enormous influence. (Many ballet lovers consider Prokofiev's *Romeo and Juliet* one of the most beautiful works in the repertoire, both in its music and its choreography — and not just because he accomplished what Tchaikovsky wanted to but never managed. Prokofiev's musical style manages to be both Russian and European at the same time, a seamless blend of the old and new. Or as one biographer puts it, Prokofiev "stood with one leg in Moscow and one in Paris" — which gives you some idea of just how big a genius he is.)

DIAGHILEV FIRST MET STRAVINSKY because he'd heard one of his little orchestral pieces, *Fireworks*, and liked it so much he asked the composer to write him a ballet for a new company of dancers he was putting together for performances in Paris. The company became the famed *Ballets Russes* and the ballet was Stravinsky's *L'Oiseaux du feu*, or *The Firebird*. (In Russian, *Zhar Ptitsa*.)[4]

Choreographed by Michel Fokine, who'd been a dancer with the Imperial Ballet before becoming a great choreographer, *The Firebird* caused a sensation in the 1910 season in Paris. Some people thought it was wildly exciting, but most just thought it was strange to look at and difficult to listen to, with its odd rhythms and discordant harmonies. (Audiences in those days had a hard time adjusting to Stravinsky. One American reviewer, writing about a Boston performance in 1914, says "In his *Fireworks*, Stravinsky hurls a whole orchestra at the head of the public, and calls it music. ... What some of the brass dissonances meant, we could not imagine, unless the man who lit the pieces had burned his fingers and made a few resultant remarks." Oh,

---

4 Stravinsky seems to have had a thing for fire. As a small boy, be probably played with matches.

75

they like to be clever, those critics. Another, writing in the New York *Sun* in 1937, confidently predicts: "It is probable that much, if not most, of Stravinsky's music will enjoy brief existence." Don't let this guy manage your stock portfolio.)

TWO DANCERS, PAVLOVA AND NIJINSKY, both trained at the Imperial Ballet in St. Petersburg, joined Diaghilev's *Ballets Russes* in the early days and went on to become two of the greatest dancers the world of ballet has ever seen. Maybe you've heard of them.

ANNA PAVLOVA WAS BORN IN 1881 and knew from the time she saw Tchaikovsky's *Sleeping Beauty* at the Imperial as an eight-year-old girl that she wanted to become a ballerina. And even though she was a little scrawny and had the wrong kind of feet, she worked and worked and practised hard every day and eventually became one of the best and most popular ballerinas the world has ever seen. (And if all that isn't a dangerous inspiration for little girls and their stage mothers everywhere, I don't know what is.) She even had a fancy dessert, Kiwifruit Pavlova, named after her.[5]

After years of practice, Pavlova joined the Imperial Ballet in 1899 and soon became its *prima ballerina*. It was for her that Fokine created what became her most famous work, *The Dying Swan*, set to music of Saint-Saëns. She danced it all over the world and it made her famous. And, as much as *Swan Lake*, it's done a pretty good PR job for swans in the world of ballet.

Ballet loves swans because they're soft and white and beautiful and graceful, and they have lovely long arching necks. Swans don't actually have long elegant legs and dainty feet — like ducks, their legs are skinny and crooked and their feet are big splayed webbed things — but artistic licence has long ago

---

[5] The great Australian coloratura soprano Nellie Melba, of course, also had a dessert named after her, Peach Melba. (And also Melba toast.) What is it about folks Down Under that they like naming food after people?

76

Pavlova and her dog get their just desserts

decreed otherwise. Funny, though, you never see many ballets about ducks, only swans. Must be the necks.

Pavlova danced only one season, 1909, with *Les Ballets Russes*. After that, she left and went out on her own. She and Diaghilev didn't get along very well, she was always jealous of Nijinsky and, truth be told, she didn't much like Stravinsky's music. All in all, it was not what you'd call a good combination.

More than anyone else, Pavlova brought ballet to the people, and the people adored her. Over the course of about 15 years of her solo career, Pavlova logged about 350,000 miles (that's about 564,000 kilometres) travelling the world and performing. And she did all of this schlepping around, remember, in the days before commercial air travel. In 1914, she married Victor Dandré, her manager/accompanist, though they kept the marriage secret for years. She didn't want to disappoint her fans. They kept a little home in London but were hardly ever there. It's now the Pavlova Museum. If she had a pet pooch, I guess it would be known as Pavlova's dog.

Because she wasn't as athletic as some of the Italian superstar ballerinas and her feet weren't ideally suited to *pointe* work, Pavlova compensated by putting stiff leather under the arches of her shoes and flattening the toe boxes to make them bigger. Oh, some called it cheating, but nowadays it's pretty much the standard design for *pointe* shoes. Pavlova wasn't without her vanity, though — she had all her photos retouched to make her feet look smaller and more dainty.

All those years on the road, sleeping on trains and in hotel rooms, eventually took their toll. Pavlova died in 1931 of pleurisy, after refusing an operation that might have saved her life but would have meant she'd never dance again. Legend has it her dying words were, "Get my swan costume ready." She probably stayed up nights thinking of that one.

VASLAV NIJINSKY WAS BORN IN 1889 and, like Pavlova, knew from childhood that he wanted to become a great dancer. He likewise studied at the Imperial Ballet and, while still a student, made his stage debut in 1906 in a *pas de huit* inserted into a production of Mozart's *Don Giovanni*, supporting the ballerina Vera Trefilova. A week later, for a repeat performance, Trefilova was replaced by Pavlova, marking the first time the two great dancers ever performed together. But theirs was never a very harmonious partnership. Too much ego on both sides. (Some scholars insist the *pas de huit* was actually a *pas de quatre*. Anyway, it was a bunch of dancers.)

Although he was a fabulously talented dancer and excelled in music, other school subjects were not Nijinsky's strong suit. In 1907 he flunked his final history exam, which would have prevented him from graduating if his history teacher hadn't convinced the school authorities to let Nijinsky write a makeover exam, which the teacher himself set and for which he personally coached his pupil. In other words, they cheated. Hey, if it works for football and basketball players, why not dancers?

Nijinsky was short — only 5'4" — but he was wiry, muscular and graceful, and had a beautiful, expressive face. One of his most famous roles was as the little faun in a ballet version of Debussy's *L'Après-midi d'un faun.*

IN 1908, WHEN HE WAS 20, Nijinsky met Diaghilev, who was about twice his age and immediately took him back to the Europa Hotel and seduced him — even though Nijinsky was clearly having an affair at the time with Prince Pavel Dimitrievitch Lvov, who'd introduced them. (Diaghilev was in a relationship at the time with his secretary, Alexis Mavrine, so maybe he thought that somehow made it OK.)

Nijinsky and Diaghilev didn't stay lovers although their professional relationship continued, and in fact Nijinsky's fling with Lvov ended soon thereafter. They just weren't happy together. (As one biographer rather tactfully puts it, "Nijinsky was small in a part where size is usually admired." He had small feet, too.)

Nijinsky obviously swung both ways, although he seems

ultimately to have preferred women. His first sex with a woman — a working girl visiting Prince Lvov's house — was, however, apparently a disappointment. She scared him — or so he later told his wife, Romola. Isn't it nice when couples are close? [6]

AFTER *THE FIREBIRD*, Nijinsky also danced in Stravinsky's next work, in 1911, *Petrushka* — not strictly a ballet, but a stage work with movement and dancing (Stravinsky called it a "burlesque"), and another one of those puppet-come-to-life stories. Believe it or not, it had started out as a piano concerto, but Diaghilev soon fixed that. At its premiere and even in later performances, critics and audiences didn't know what to make of that one, either ("an incomprehensible phantasmagoria of tone," *New York Times*, 1923; "a disjointed series of funny sounds, squeaks and squawks," *New York Tribune*, 1923).

BUT THAT WAS NOTHING compared to the *scandale* of the opening night of *Le Sacre du Printemps* (*The Rite of Spring*), a *tableaux* of primitive pagan ritual that one wag christened *Massacre du Printemps*. From the moment of its opening bars, with a lonely bassoon absurdly high in its register (even way above the oboe, which is relatively speaking down in its boots), you can hear you're in for something unusual. And that's before all the sexy pounding rhythmic stuff. Music's never quite been the same since. [7]

What had started on that May evening in Paris in 1913 as mere (mere!) boos and hisses from the audience pretty soon developed into a full-scale riot in the seats, with people slapping and punching each other, screaming, tearing up the seats and generally behaving like the teen crowd at a punk concert. (Stravinsky was obviously ahead of his time.) Trying to calm the crowd, Diaghilev had the stagehands flash the lights on an off,

---

[6] Nijinsky's sister, Bronislava, believes the story but thinks it happened somewhere else. Whatever.

[7] Bassoonists love the opening of *Le Sacre*. They hardly ever get to be on top.

but I guess that only got them more riled up. (It's the same at punk concerts.)[8]

Ironically, pretty soon the audience was making so much noise they couldn't have heard the music anyway, but by then things had gotten well and truly out of hand. Poor old Nijinksy, who'd choreographed the work as well as dancing in it, had to resort to stamping his feet and shouting out beat numbers, trying to keep the dancers together. It was a lost cause.

The rhythms in *Le Sacre* are really tricky. There are bits in the final movement, *Danse Sacrale*, where Stravinsky himself, whenever he conducted it, would burp quietly on the downbeat, just to keep on track.[9]

BOTH THEN AND LATER, the critics, as you can imagine, had a field day:

"The most dissonant and the most discordant composition yet written."
— *Le Temps*, Paris, 1913
"baffles verbal description ... hideous ..."
— *Musical Times*, London, 1913.
" ... more of an affliction than a privilege."
— Philadelphia *Evening Bulletin*, 1922.
"... horrible ..."
— Philadelphia *Public Ledger*, 1922.

And my personal favorite, with extra points for rhyming, from the Boston Herald in 1924:

---

[8] For some of the time he was writing *Le Sacre*, Stravinsky had a terrible toothache. That probably explains a lot.

[9] The term "pagan," by the way, was originally an insult the early Christians hurled at rival religious beliefs. It translates, roughly speaking, as "bumpkin" or "yokel" or "rube." So much for "love thy neighbor."

Who wrote this fiendish *Rite of Spring*,
What right had he to write the thing,
Against our helpless ears to fling
Its crash, clash, cling, clang, bing, bang, bing?

And then to call it *Rite of Spring*,
The season when on joyous wing
The birds melodious carols sing
And harmony's in everything!

He who could write the *Rite of Spring*.
If I be right, by right should swing!

OF COURSE, IT WASN'T JUST the music that got audiences so riled — it was the scandalous eroticism of the subject-matter, and (for those days, anyway) the graphic nature with which it was displayed. And of course it didn't help that Nijinsky himself made a rude gesture ("too audacious and too intimate," as Stravinsky later put it) at the audience. People tend to resent that sort of thing.

LATER IN LIFE NIJINSKY, sad to say, went a little loopy and had to be committed to an asylum. It wasn't just dancing to Stravinsky's music that sent him around the bend, but I'm sure it didn't help. You try counting all those polyrhythms and keeping on the beat — they'd drive anyone crazy!

STRAVINSKY WENT ON TO WRITE other ballets and stage works with movement, including *L'Histoire du Soldat*, in 1918, an anti-war piece for narrator, dancer and a small group of instruments, and *Jeux de cartes* (*A Game of Cards*, cleverly subtitled "a ballet in three deals").

He also wrote and a bunch of others the titles of which escape me right now (you can look them up yourself — do I have to do *everything* myself?). But whatever their merits, artistic or otherwise, none of them came even close to matching the impact, both artistic and social, of *Le Sacre du Printemps*.

With that work alone, you might say, Stravinsky proved he had the *Rite* stuff.

Line dancing meets la volta

ALL MOD CONS

SINCE *LE SACRE*, the world of dance has been getting more and more exotic, erotic and adventuresome. Even so-called "classical" ballet, although it still remains firmly connected to those formal poses and positions of its long-ago roots, is in many ways a far cry from what Lully and Beauchamps — or even Tchaikovsky and Petipa — would recognize.

America has had a hand in this, as it often does, and American connections to classical ballet go back a respectable distance. In the 19th century, an American dancer with the entirely appropriate name of George Washington Smith danced as Albrecht in *Giselle* in a production in Paris, opposite Fanny Elssler. Elssler also toured the United States, as did other European stars, including Anna Pavlova and the Diaghilev Ballet.

The 1910s and '20s produced the brief but notable career of Isadora Duncan, an American dancer/choreographer who was as talented as she was eccentric. Or eccentric as she was talented. Anyway, she was both. Part flapper, part Serious Artist, part nutbar, Isadora Duncan liked to dance barefoot in flowing robes, and there's no doubt her style and energy had an important influence on the development of modern dance.

She might have had an even bigger influence if she hadn't died tragically, and very suddenly, in 1927. On tour in France, she decided to go for a motorcar ride near Nice, but as she was getting into the car her long scarf got caught up in the spokes of one of the wheels. As soon as the car started rolling, the scarf pulled taut and broke her neck. This is a very good reason not to have spoked wheels, or not to wear scarves, or at least not to have both together.

MICHEL FOKINE WAS PART OF THE CROWD of Russian dancers and choreographers who went to the U.S. after the First World War and the Russian Revolution — and who could blame them for wanting to get away from all that? Many of them settled in New York — which is where the Russian Tea Room gets its name, by the way. Fokine helped establish a New York company in the 1920s and '30s that did some good work, but in some ways he never really got the hang of his new home. His ballet *Thunder Bird*, for instance, although based on Aztec mythology, uses music by Russian composers, including Borodin and Glinka. This sort of thing rarely works — though, to be fair, I have no idea what Aztec music actually sounds like, and who knows where Fokine might have been able to find some? Not the kind of thing you can go to the store and buy in a recording, probably.

IN THE 1930S, THE IMPRESARIO LINCOLN KIRSTEIN and others persuaded George Balanchine (born Georgi Balanchivadze) to come to the U.S. and start a company in New York. They opened the School of American Ballet in 1934, coincidentally in a Manhattan studio that had once belonged to Isadora Duncan. (Balanchine was a big fan of Ginger Rogers, whom he'd seen dancing in some of those movies with Fred Astaire. Maybe Balanchine hoped that by going to America he'd get a chance to meet her.)

Although Balanchine knew how to tell a story in dance, he much preferred abstract works that were more like expressions of pure movement, such as his ballets *Serenade* or *Mozartiana*. ("Why should we do Shakespeare?" he once said. "Shakespeare's already done Shakespeare.") Sometimes his ideas came from the strangest places. Once in rehearsal for *Serenade*, when a dancer fell down, he decided to work that into the piece. Hey, whatever works.

Balanchine wasn't just a highbrow *artiste*. He also did a lot of work on Broadway, choreographing such productions as *On Your Toes* and *Babes in Arms*, and in Hollywood films such as *Goldwyn Follies*. (He also did that little circus number for elephants with Stravinksy, you'll remember.)

After the Second World War, in 1946, Balanchine and Kirstein formed a new group called the Ballet Society, which later became the New York City Ballet, which continues to be an important and influential company. After Balanchine, the chief choreographers were Jerome Robbins (another crossover Broadway guy) and Peter Martins.

ANOTHER INFLUENTIAL AMERICAN DANCER and choreographer of the early 20th century was Martha Graham, whose performances were both energetic and controversial. (Like Balanchine and Robbins, she also had showbiz connections, having taught movement to such stars as Bette Davis and Gregory Peck.)

Graham was an "earthy" dancer in many senses of the word. her dances were often sensual and frankly erotic, and she was known also for her powerful "floor work," at a time when the ballet ideal was still one of dancers who floated through the air as if weightless. She created dances to the music of such important Amercian composers as Aaron Copland and Samuel Barber (again, no relation to me, alas).

Her work was often artistically daring and shocking. In her 1946 dance *Cave of the Heart*, for instance, she plays a crazed Medea who consumes her own entrails. Well, give her credit. That kind of thing takes guts.

SPEAKING OF RUSSIANS, Latvian-born Mikhail Baryshnikov defected from Soviet Russia in 1974, at the airport in Toronto while on a North American tour. He went on to dance at both the American Ballet Theater and the New York City Ballet, and even once starred in a Hollywood movie about, you guessed it, a Russian dancer who defected. (As opposed to a defective Russian dancer, which is something else again.)

Speaking of defecting Russians, Baryshnikov was following in the footsteps, as it were, of Rudolf Nureyev, the son of Russian peasants who danced with the Kirov Ballet before defecting to the West when the company was on tour to Paris.[1]

Nureyev has been called the Nijinsky of his generation — a flamboyant, powerful dancer with a powerful ego to match. He liked publicity, he liked being seen with rich and famous celebrities and he could swear like a sailor on shore leave. Among his favorite dancing partners were Margot Fonteyn and Karen Kain, when she was principal ballerina of the National Ballet of Canada.

CANADA HAS TWO MAJOR ballet companies — the Royal Winnipeg Ballet, founded by Gwyneth Lloyd and Betty Farrally, and the National Ballet, founded by former Sadler's Wells dancer Celia Franca. Founded in 1939, the RWB is not only the older of the two, but has the distinction of being the oldest continuously running ballet company in North America. Franca was also instrumental in introducing Western classical ballet to China, which has been turning out top-notch ballet dancers ever since.

NURYEV, BLANCHINE, GRAHAM and a host of others help maintain the discipline and artistry of the past, but often with a fresh, new perspective. Even today, little girls and boys in towns and cities all over the world stand at the *barre* in front of mirrors practising their pliés and arabesques and dreaming of swans and sugar-plum fairies.

AND IN THE FIELD of what's called "modern" dance, we're in an area where, like that old Cole Porter song, pretty much anything goes. Ballet, jazz, burlesque, mime, gymnastics, acrobatics — it's

---

[1] You'd think the Soviets would have learned not to let their dancers go on tour, but they never did. Now, of course, it doesn't matter so much.

all being combined into one big, broad, expressive style. Even moves you might before have seen only from "exotic" nightclub dancers (oh, you know the ones — don't try to pretend you don't) you'll now see on stage, although sometimes it seems to go a little too far. One "performance artist" (one hesitates to call her a dancer) a few years ago caused quite a stir by walking onto the stage and peeing into a bucket. That's it — that was her show. Well, she got lots of attention, anyway, but I wonder where she is today?

AND JUST AS MAZURKAS and Morris dancing and other dances of the ordinary folks sometimes have made their way into the highbrow ballet, modern dance today borrows bits and pieces from all sorts of popular forms, from mambos to mosh pits to (God help us) country-and-western line dancing.

In fact, it's really not much of a stretch to see the connection between modern line dancing and the formal, rigid floor patterns danced at the 16th-century French court. Funny how everything connects, isn't it? And with that, you might say, the world of ballet and dance has come full circle.

INDEX

ABOUT THE AUTHOR

DAVID BARBER is a journalist and musician and the author of seven previous books of musical history and humor. Formerly entertainment editor of the Kingston *Whig-Standard* and editor of *Broadcast Week* magazine at the Toronto *Globe and Mail*, he is now a freelance journalist in Toronto. As a composer, his works include two symphonies, a jazz mass based on the music of Dave Brubeck, a *Requiem*, several short choral and chamber works and various vocal-jazz arrangements. An avid kayaker and reader of detective mysteries, he also enjoys singing with his vocal-jazz group, Barber & the Sevilles.

David's web site is at: www.bachbeethoven.com

ABOUT THE CARTOONIST

DAVE DONALD can't remember when he didn't scrawl his little marks on most surfaces, so it doesn't come as much of a surprise that he now makes a living doing just that. He is currently balancing a steady job as an art director at a Toronto magazine with his more abstruse pursuits. This book represents Dave's seventh illustrative collaboration with David Barber.

Tutus, Tights and Tiptoes:
Ballet History As It Ought to Be Taught

Published in Canada by

SOUND AND VISION
359 Riverdale Avenue
Toronto, Canada M4J 1A4
www.soundandvision.com

First printing, September 2000
1 3 5 7 9 11 - printings - 12 10 8 6 4 2

Canadian Cataloguing in Publication Data

Barber, David W. (David William), 1958-
Tutus, tights and tiptoes: ballet history as it ought to be taught

ISBN 0-920151-30-2

1. Ballet - Humor. I. Donald, David C. II. Title
GV1787.B288 2000   792.8'02'07   C99-931900-0

Typeset in Caslon 540 and Caslon 3
Printed and bound in Canada

Other Sound And Vision books by David W. Barber,
with cartoons by Dave Donald:

A Musician's Dictionary
preface by Yehudi Menhuin
ISBN 0-920151-21-3

Bach, Beethoven and the Boys
Music History as It Ought to Be Taught
preface by Anthony Burgess
ISBN 0-920151-10-8

When the Fat Lady Sings
Opera History as It Ought to Be Taught
preface by Maureen Forrester
ISBN 0-920151-34-5

If It Ain't Baroque
More Music History as It Ought to Be Taught
ISBN 0-920151-15-9

Getting a Handel on Messiah
preface by Trevor Pinnock
ISBN 0-920151-17-5

Tenors, Tantrums and Trills
An Opera Dictionary from Aida to Zzzz
ISBN 0-920151-19-1

by David W. Barber:

Better Than It Sounds
A Dictionary of Humorous Musical Quotations
ISBN 0-920151-22-1

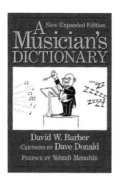

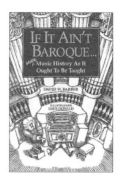

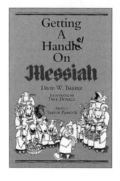

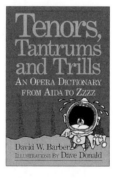

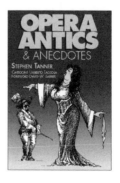

Other musical humor books from Sound And Vision:

The Thing I've Played With The Most
Prof. Anthon E. Darling Discusses His Favourite Instrument
by David E. Walden, cartoons Mike Duncan
foreword Dave Boadfoot
ISBN 0-920151-35-3

1812 and All That
A Concise History of Music from 30,000 BC to the Millennium
by Lawrence Leonard, cartoons Emma Bebbington
ISBN 0-920151-33-7

Opera Antics & Anecdotes
by Stephen Tanner, cartoons Umberto Tàccola
foreword David W. Barber
ISBN 0-920151-32-9

How To Listen To Modern Music
Without Earplugs
by David E. Walden, cartoons Mike Duncan
foreword Bramwell Tovey
ISBN 0-920151-31-0

The Composers
A Hystery of Music
by Kevin Reeves, preface Daniel Taylor
ISBN 0-920151-29-9

A Working Musician's Joke Book
by Daniel G. Theaker, cartoons Mike Freen
preface David Barber
ISBN 0-920151-23-X

How To Stay Awake
During Anybody's Second Movement
by David E. Walden, cartoons Mike Duncan
preface Charlie Farquharson
ISBN 0-920151-20-5

Love Lives of the Great Composers
From Gesualdo to Wagner
by Basil Howitt
ISBN 0-920151-18-3

I Wanna Be Sedated
Pop Music in the Seventies
by Phil Dellio & Scott Woods, cartoons Dave Prothero
preface Chuck Eddy
ISBN 0-920151-16-7

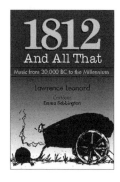

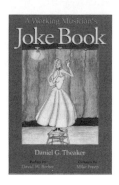

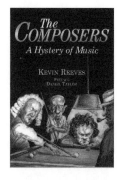

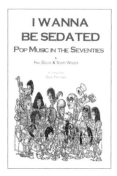

NOTE FROM THE PUBLISHER

If you have any comments on this book or any other book we publish or if you would like a catalogue, please write to us at:

Sound And Vision, 359 Riverdale Avenue,

Toronto, Canada M4J 1A4.

email: musicbooks@soundandvision.com

Or visit our Web site at: **www.soundandvision.com**. We would really like to hear from you.

We are always looking for original books to publish. If you have an idea or manuscript that is in the genre of musical humor, please contact us at our address. Thank you for purchasing or borrowing this book.

DATE DUE